Social Research Perspectives

Occasional Reports on Current Topics

D1611917

11

Risk Acceptability According to the Social Sciences

by Mary Douglas

RUSSELL SAGE FOUNDATION   NEW YORK

The Russell Sage Foundation

Library of Congress Cataloging-in-Publication Data

Douglas, Mary Tew.
  Risk acceptability according to the social sciences.

  (Social research perspectives: occasional reports
on current topics ; 11)
  Bibliography: p.
  1. Risk perception—Social aspects. I. Title.
II. Series: Social research perspectives; 11.
H91.D67 1985   304   85-60758
ISBN 0-87154-211-0

NOTICE of series title change: *Social Research Perspectives* is a new title for the *Social Science Frontiers* series (volumes 1–9 published 1969–1977). The numbering of *Perspectives* volumes is a continuation of the *Frontiers* numbering.

10 9 8 7 6 5 4 3 2 1

Social Research Perspectives

Occasional Reports on Current Topics
from the Russell Sage Foundation

The *Social Research Perspectives* series revives a special format
used by the Russell Sage Foundation for nine volumes published
from 1969 to 1977 under the series title, *Social Science Frontiers*.
The *Frontiers* series established itself as a valuable source of information about significant developments in the social sciences.

With the re-named *Perspectives* series, we again provide a timely,
flexible, and accessible outlet for the products of ongoing social
research—from literature reviews to explorations of emerging issues and new methodologies; from summaries of current policy to
agendas for future study and action.

The following *Frontiers* titles are still available:

5 *The Corporate Social Audit,* by Raymond A. Bauer and Dan
   H. Fenn, Jr. (1972)

7 *Social Forecasting Methodology: Suggestions for Research,* by
   Daniel P. Harrison (1976)

8 *The Vulnerable Age Phenomenon,* by Michael Inbar (1976)

9 *Work and Family in the United States: A Critical Review and
   Agenda for Research and Policy,* by Rosabeth Moss Kanter
   (1977)

Now available in the *Perspectives* series:

10 *Your Time Will Come: The Law of Age Discrimination and
    Mandatory Retirement,* by Lawrence M. Friedman

Contents

Originally this was intended as a review of the literature on social influences on risk perception. However, it proved difficult to achieve the usual form of a literature review. When there is a large, focused body of work to be abstracted, various outlying areas and innovations can be related within a single framework. In this case the relevant work is found entirely in the outlying areas, and the central core of interest in social influences on risk perception is missing. At the same time a very significant body of work views risk perception as an individual and not as a social phenomenon. To start with, surveying the state of the art in that substantial field would take all the time and attention away from the set project since it turns out that that art is in no state at all. The best strategy seems to be to use the question of risk acceptability to make the case for focusing on social factors as strongly as possible. With the change of title, it becomes obviously necessary to point to the scattered, exceptional places where this focus is employed. It seems that the neglect of culture is so systematic and so entrenched that nothing less than a large upheaval in the social sciences would bring about a change.

1

The subject matter of these pages is strictly described by the title. It is not about risks. Those who want to learn about the risks we face in the present day are advised to read no further. It is not about risk management. Those who want to learn how to handle risks of any kind should save their time and read no more. These notes are about perception as treated in the various social sciences, and the particular focus is upon risk perception according to the social sciences.

Purity and Danger (Douglas 1966) presented an anthropological approach to human cognition which this volume develops. The argument is that humans pay attention to a particular pattern of disasters, treating them as omens or punishments. On this argument there would always be a mutual adaptation of views about natural dangers and views about how society works: Rewards and punishments are stored in the environment. *Purity and Danger* was well received except for the damning reservation that its argument docs not apply to enlightened Western society.

In 1978 Aaron Wildavsky, then president of the Russell Sage Foundation, inquired whether anthropology made its cultural analyses only for tribal peoples and ancient civilizations. Are we moderns always exempted from its hypotheses? He was concerned to interpret a cultural change in contemporary America: the new awareness of technological dangers. It was a privilege to collaborate with him in working out the argument of *Risk and Culture* (Douglas and Wildavsky 1982). Although both books stand in the respectable tradition of Durkheim and Mauss, *Risk and Culture* has struck competent reviewers as either novel or outrageous, and always as difficult. So it seemed important to examine the contrary intellectual tide against whose currents the argument about social influences on cognition has so little force. Hence the intended literature review. Close inspection reveals no tide, but some inertia; no contrary currents, but some timidity.

Sometimes the curiosity of scholars fastens steadily upon certain formulations and problems, to the neglect of others. There is enough agreement among psychologists that when this happens there is nothing haphazard about it. The sociology of perception (which includes the history, philosophy, and sociology of science and the sociology of everyday knowledge) is especially interested in persisting gaps in information. We may expect some random patches of inattention because of the impossibility of attending to everything at once. But regularly scheduled obliviousness is more intriguing. Persistent shortsightedness, selectivity, and tolerated contradiction are usually not so much signs of perceptual weakness as signs of strong intention to protect certain values and their accompanying institutional forms. The current gaps in research in risk perception can be used as a paradigmatic example. Intellectual activity takes place in history. No way of knowing is privileged from contemporary cultural pressures. Gaps and contradictions in a system of thought are a good guide to the institutional fabric which supports it and to which it gives life.

The professional discussion of cognition and choice has no sustained theorizing about the social influences which select particular risks for public attention. Yet it is hard to maintain seriously that perception of risk is private. Nor can it be maintained that culture is so static that it can be bracketed away. Large cultural changes since 1969 are precisely the problem. The social bases of credibility need to be systematically studied, but because the individual perceiver is supposed to be out on his own, the culturally constructed lines between reality and fiction and between nature and culture are treated as self-evident. In consequence, risk perception studies stay within the very confines they are instituted to transcend.

With no link between cultural analysis and cognitive science, clashes inevitably occur between theory and evidence. Since the theory is not being radically adjusted, irrationality tends to be invoked to protect the too narrow definition of rationality. So instead of a sociological, cultural, and ethical theory of human judgment, there is an unintended emphasis on perceptual pathology.

Regrettably, this report cannot claim completeness or even up-to-dateness as it goes to press. The field to be sampled is too diverse and the project seems to have moved down one blind alley after another. The best that can be hoped is that no systematic, sociological approach to perception has been overlooked.

Chapter 1 names the moral issues which make risk perception an important policy matter. Justice and morality in risk-taking are much discussed by philosophers, but little is said about how a given set of moral principles affects perception of risk. Chapter 2 describes the emergence of a new subdiscipline dedicated to the perception of risk—its origins in ecology, psychology, and economics. Chapter 3 discusses psychology's approaches to risk perception and its tendency to neglect the social dimension. Chapter

4 considers the place of risk in the theory of choice. This is the dominant paradigm of Western social thought. Its inability to deal with moral ends somewhat accounts for the theoretical weaknesses of the new subdiscipline which is meant to interpret a strong moral response on the part of the public. From chapters 1 through 4 the notes move further and further away from real-world concerns toward pure theory. Chapter 5 makes a new start. It explains how moral judgment is involved with risk perception, even in our own society. From there on, in chapters 6, 7, 8, and 9, the developing theme is how perception of risks is encoded in social institutions. The trouble is that the constructive approach is made from anthropology, and therefore with not enough expertise for analyzing contemporary society.

Recently, some severe criticisms of science and the social sciences have appeared. They unfold grim tales of inquiry deflected by concern for professional interests or for the sake of political commitments, even for the sheer personal aggrandizement of a researcher. This book presents a very different kind of story from that of Stephen Jay Gould (1981) on biological determinism harnessed to serve racial supremacy, or from that of Edith Efron (1984) on unscrupulous misrepresentations of toxicity in research on carcinogens. For one thing, finagling is nowhere suspected. Furthermore, the systematic bias which is being reported here is the same whatever the political allegiance. It is a bias incorporated into the structure of the social science disciplines, somewhat in the same way as Joseph Gusfield (1981) shows that the attraction of locating the fault for road accidents in drunken driving is structurally incorporated in the legal and insurance professions. These criticisms of research have a straightforward moral lesson: Strive for more perfect objectivity. But in the case of risk perception, the bias is partly due to a fierce dedication to objectivity which has demarcated areas where no one goes for fear of betraying it. The failing is rather the timidity which assumes that it is impossible to set up an objective conceptual framework that will encompass the relation of mind to social commitments. Consequently, the final thrust of this book is not to remonstrate, but to open an approach to risk perception which has not been given a chance. For it is well said by Tom Nagel (1980) that to give up the pursuit of an objective conception of the mind because it cannot be complete would be like giving up axiomatization in mathematics because it cannot be complete.

4

Chapter 1　Moral Issues in Risk Acceptability

Summary: This chapter indicates the risk issues that involve social justice and considers the neglect of that part of the topic of risk acceptability.

In every generation one or another branch of the social sciences is put on the witness stand to be interrogated about drastic problems—famine or economic recession, the causes of war or crime. For the last decade and more, such urgent questions have been about the risks of new technology. The fears and conscience of Western industrial nations have been roused by nuclear radiation, chemical wastes, asbestos and lead poisoning. In response, an important new subdiscipline of the social sciences has emerged which specifically addresses questions asked by industry and government about the public perception of risk. (See Table 1 on page 7.)

The public reception of any policy for risks will depend on standardized public ideas about justice. It is often held that perception of risk is directed by issues of fairness. The more that institutions depend upon personal commitment rather than upon coercion, the more explicitly they are monitored for fairness. The threshold of risk acceptability in the workplace is lowered when the workers consider themselves exploited. Awareness of medical risks is heightened if the medical profession is suspected of malpractice. Whether the sharper sensitivity to risks causes individuals to be more prudent in avoiding them is another matter.

Rawl's concept of justice as fairness (1971), which lies at the basis of his moral philosophy, allows for cultural and social variation in concepts of fairness. But these variations would influence perception of risk. Furthermore, the variation in values corresponds to variation in possible kinds of organization. Selsnick (1969) found that fairness means one thing to unskilled manual workers (fairness as equal treatment for all) and another to clerical, professional, and management cadres (fairness as fair recognition of individual ability). Fairness as equality would seem appropriate in a highly ascriptive system with no opportunities for personal advancement and some expectations from collective bargaining; fairness as rewards for merit would be appealing to persons faced with opportunities for promotion. This is important if the claim is true that "the best predictor of opposition to nuclear energy is the belief that American society is unjust" (Rothman and Lichter 1982).

In some professional analyses the existing allocation of risks is taken to imply an accepted norm of distributive justice sustaining the moral fabric of society. Those who are in the more favored sectors of the community as regards the incidence of morbidity and mortality rates may be tempted not to think too deeply about its inequities. However, others would judge a society inequitable that regularly exposes a large percentage of its population to much higher risks than the fortunate top 10 percent.

The Poor Risk More

A cursory look at the labor and health statistics for the United States shows that, below a certain level, income is a good predictor of relative exposure to risks of most kinds. The percentage of persons who are unable through chronic ill health to carry on their major activity declines as income rises. In 1976–77 income had a greater impact than race upon a person's limitation of activity, but the death rates for disadvantaged minorities in 1977 were higher than for whites at all age levels until age 80 (U.S. Department of Health and Human Services 1980a:2).Blue-collar workers reported a rate of 40.6 persons injured per 100 currently employed. An average of 21 percent of blue-collar workers were injured at work, and 19.89 percent of farm workers, compared with 5.1 percent of white-collar workers. At incomes less than $10,000, the picture worsens (U.S. Department of Health and Human Services 1980b).

Table 1   Growth of Research in Risk Perception

I. RESEARCH INSTITUTIONS

Date	Institution	Chairperson
1969	NSF Technology Assessment and Risk Analysis Group, 1800 G Street N.W. Washington, DC 20550	Joshua Menkes
Early 1970s	International Institute for Applied Systems Analysis Risk Group 2361 Laxemburg, Austria	Howard Kunreuther
1976	Decision Research 1201 Oak Street Eugene, OR 97401	Robert Kates Roger Kasperson
1978–79	Institute for Risk Analysis American University Washington, DC 20016	William Rowe
1979	National Research Council 2101 Constitution Avenue N.W. Washington, DC 20418	
1979	Center for Philosophy and Public Policy University of Maryland College Park, Maryland 20742	Douglas MacLean
1980	Hudson Institute 1500 Wilson Boulevard, Suite 810 Arlington, VA 22209	Max Singer
1980	Society for Risk Analysis Oak Ridge National Laboratory Oak Ridge, TN 37830	Robert B. Cumming
1981	Institute of Resource Ecology University of British Columbia Vancouver, B.C., Canada	C. S. Holling
	Technology Assessment Section System Analysis Division Joint Research Center Commission of the European Communities I-21020 Ispra (Varese), Italy	Harry Otway
	Center for Technology and Policy Studies P.O. Box 541, 7300 AM Apeldoorn, Holland	P. J. M. Stallen

7

Table 1 Growth of Research in Risk Perception (continued)

II. CONFERENCES

Date	Organizer	Sponsor	Title	Chairperson
May 1980	Banbury Center, Cold Spring Harbor Labs Cold Spring Harbor, N.Y. 11724	EPA, Exxon Foundation, International Life Sciences Institute	Product Labeling and Health Risk	Louis A. Morris Michael B. Mazis Ivan Barofsky
October 1980	Oregon Decision Research Center Eugene, Oregon	Office of Naval Research	Risk Perception Workshop	Paul Slovic
April 22–24, 1981	Science Application, Inc. Watsonville, California	Electric Power Research Institute	Public Perception of Risk	Kenneth Arrow
June 1–3, 1981	Society for Risk Analysis Bethesda, Maryland	Alfred P. Sloan Foundation, EPA, Nuclear Regulatory Commission, Board on Toxicology and Environmental Health, Assembly for Behavorial and Social Sciences, NAS/NRS, World Health Organization	International Workshop on the Analysis of Actual Versus Perceived Risks	Norton Nelson

8

Date	Location	Sponsor	Title	Organizer
June 22–26, 1981	International Institute for Applied Systems Analysis, Laxemburg, Austria	IIASA	Decision Processes and Institutional Aspects of Risk	Howard Kunreuther
June 22–26, 1981	University of British Columbia, Vancouver, B.C., Canada	University of British Columbia	Adoptive Behavior and the Dynamic of Surprise	C. S. Holling
September 1981	University of California, Berkeley, California	NSF	Assessment of Orientations Toward Technology	Kenneth H. Craik
June 15–17, 1982	Society for Risk Analysis, Arlington, Virginia	Nuclear Regulatory Commission, EPA Department of Energy	Workshop on Low Probability/High Consequence Risk-Analysis	Vincent Covello, Ray Walkler
July 27–29, 1983	New York University Graduate School of Public Administration, New York, New York		Summer Institute in Risk Management in Environmental Health Protection	Rae Zimmerman

9

Effects are cumulative. Excessive exposure to lead poisoning is particularly a danger for young children in poor families (largely due to household paint applied before the 1940s and to automobile emissions and made worse by iron deficiency and undernutrition) (U.S. Department of Health and Human Services 1983). Likewise the effects of tobacco smoking will be greatly exacerbated for persons whose occupations expose their lungs to irritants, which means persons who work among factory fumes and dust.

Since the present distribution of risks reflects only the present distribution of power and status, fundamental political questions are raised by the justice issue. It is well said that the technical problems of risk analysis "pale before the political difficulties raised by the basic assumption that current risk–benefit trade-offs are satisfactory" (Fischhoff et al. 1980:137). When a greater damage to a larger population can be avoided by relocating a dangerous industry to a sparsely settled area, fundamental ethical issues are raised. It is true that in a desert with a thin scattering of Indian tribes, fewer people will suffer damage. But why ever should the Indians of the American Southwest, already burdened by economic and health disadvantages, agree to be sacrificed to the greatest happiness principle? Should the price of a life be uniform for all lives? Should compensation be related to earning power? Should a young person's life be counted more than an old person's because its expected span of earning has been cut off short? The earning power principle comes into flagrant contradiction with equality. Intuitively, giving more risks to those who carry more smacks of elementary injustice. The employer's liability toward his work force includes responsibility to prevent accidents, to provide full information about occupational risks, and to ensure appropriate compensation for victims. How should his liabilities be traded off against his costs? Should it be left to his conscience? Should the decisions be regulated from above? The answers are about political, economic, and moral pressures that influence the public feeling of what is tolerable.

The question of acceptability of risk involves freedom as well as justice. Consider the workers' choice: If they are offered danger money for risky work, are they to be the sole judges of what risks they should take or should they be regulated? The freedom of the individual in liberal democracy is at issue. And when it comes to danger money, it is not clear that the riskier jobs really are the most highly compensated (Graham and Shakow 1981). The basis

10

of compensation rates is generally related to normal expectation of rewards, but what about expectations of injury? It seems that in the United States nonwhites have higher expectations of being injured at work than whites. Figures based on medical attendance show a lower rate of reported injury for nonwhites but a greater proportion of physical damage. This means that they do not trouble to turn up at the clinic for minor injuries but use it if severely incapacitated (U.S. Department of Health, Education and Welfare 1979). If a community which once heroically accepted the dangers of coal mining is now suffering the misery of unemployment, who is to tell them not to have a liquid natural gas site in their neighborhood, if they perceive it as a source of incomes and pensions? Or if a community, using its regularly instituted procedures of vote-casting, rejects or hesitates to accept a nuclear plant in its midst, what is the ethical status of an offer to buy off the opposition? What kind of community amenities can be provided that will compensate for the risks? In the time span of the bargains, will the promised benefits last longer than the risks? Has a community any inherent right to commit its future generations to heavy risks? The ethical theory on which disputants draw is in disarray.

Rights of Future Generations

Golding (1972) pours scorn on attempts to secure the ethical claims of Martians, Venusians, strange peoples on this earth, and unborn generations: "If someone finds it difficult to think of having an obligation to his unborn child, he should find it difficult to think of having an obligation towards the community of humans (humanoids?) fifty generations hence." Schwartz argues that long-range welfare policies to give benefit to future generations cannot be justified by appeal to welfare of remote unidentifiable individuals: Ethically objectionable acts must have victims (Schwartz 1979. The counterargument is made by Routley (1979) on behalf of future people. (See also Barry and Sikora 1978.)

A wider failure to think systematically about distributive justice is inherent in the most prestigious part of the conceptual apparatus of Western social thought. A sigh of relief seems to have been heard from economists when they realized that a fully subjectivized utility theory gave them an analytic tool that could not deal with absolutes or objective rights and wrongs. Dealing only with individuals' ranked preferences, the economists' subject matter was withdrawn from the political arena. The tool of comparison seemed to achieve the value-neutrality of an exact science. It took some time to accept the cost of not being able to say anything about distributive justice, but when Lionel Robbins had announced this clearly the whole topic is said to have been quietly dropped. "The attack of Robbins (1932) and others on interpersonal comparability does not distinguish between *some* comparability and *total* comparability of units, and the consequence has been the virtual elimination of distributional questions from the formal literature on welfare economics . . . " (Sen 1970:99–100). Without an intellectually respectable way of discussing justice, there is no way of discussing the acceptability of risk, as most policy issues concerning risk raise grave problems of justice.

Writers on risk acceptability tend to content themselves with a perfunctory tribute to moral issues or with inventories of ethical problems.

Salute to Moral Principles

Fischhoff et al. (1980) are emphatic that values affect acceptability: the "search for an 'objective method' for solving problems of acceptable risk is doomed to failure and may blind the searchers to the value-laden assumptions they are making . . . not only does each approach fail to give a definitive answer, but it is predisposed to representing particular interests and recommending particular solutions. Hence, choice of a method is a political decision with a distinct message about who should rule and what should matter. . . . The controlling factor in many acceptable-risk decisions is how the problem is defined." They recommend making explicit the limitations of methods of analysis, facilitating consideration of risk problems within existing democratic institutions, clarifying government involvement, and strengthening social mechanisms for controlling risks. While making faultless recommendations for policymakers, this team cannot see any way of bringing their topic, risk-acceptability, within the scope of analysis by any of the methods they discuss. Objectivity about values is impossible.

Kasperson (1980) provides an excellent preliminary inventory of ethical statements, official and unofficial, on waste management. Rather than focus on the concepts of justice and fairness, MacLean (1982) prefers the concept of consent as a principle for justifying centralized decisions which impose risk. MacLean proposes an intrinsic link between his concept of consent and rationality: "At one end, consent is vivid, actual and explicit, and the role of rationality in understanding the normative force of this kind of consent is present but minimal. As we move toward the other end of the continuum, consent becomes less explicit, more indirect, even entirely hypothetical, and the concept of rationality correspondingly becomes richer and takes on a more important normative role." MacLean questions the usefulness of "justice, rights, or efficiency" as principles of justifying centralized decisions.

But justice should not be separated from the theory of knowledge. Future generations are likely to see the present intellectual impasse as the consequence which tends to follow when a theoretical discipline (in this case the theory of rational behavior) has generated a powerful technology of analysis which in turn supports the intricate machinery of administration on which the contemporary society depends. It is difficult to resist the bias which is inculcated with social norms. Isolated criticisms of the limitations of the theory of rational choice are useless: It is too deeply embedded in our institutions. Any improvements will have to be incremental on its existing base. No wonder risk perception studies avoid deep issues.

The dialogue about risk and justice tends to be conducted in two languages: traditional English rhetoric on behalf of regulation and mathematical language on behalf of principles of free choice. This is reminiscent of a medieval law court in which the native plaintiffs made their vernacular requests and were answered in dog Latin. The parallel case is in medical practice where the doctor speaks one language to colleagues and another to the patient. Is this an inevitable result of professionalization and does it carry an element of coercion? Those who denounce the cultural hegemony of the ruling classes would suspect that an arcane and rigid tool of analysis is used to control the discourse about risk. On the other side, the rational choice philosophers claim to use a neutral, objective conceptual scheme to solve problems by sheer power of reason. But if the conceptual tool is objective and neutral, how did it happen that its use has allowed these systematic perceptual gaps?

Where social theory fails, a new jurisprudential inquiry may help by classifying the cases and laying bare the underlying principles. Calabresi (1970) did this very successfully for the laws governing accidents, using the neutral principle of cost efficiency to reorganize the whole field. But it would be extraordinarily ingenious to organize the principles of risk distribution by tests of cost efficiency—perhaps a major philosophical triumph, but more likely an impossibility because costs can be used only within a

13

fixed scheme of valuations, whereas the issue of acceptable risk lies with the principles of valuation itself, that is, with culture.

Social justice combines three principles: needs, deserts, and equity, and each comes into some conflict with the others. A real society uses institutional conventions to work out its unique compromise. Human needs are set by social standards; the principle that some threshold of human wants should be set, below which no member of the community should be allowed to fall, may entail a redistribution. So the desert principle, which accords rightful rewards to the well-deserving, may be compromised so as to meet the needs of others; and if the needy are also undeserving, then the principle of equity is strained. These ultimate principles of community life cannot be reconciled except through assumptions inaccessible to direct inquiry, enshrined in institutions. It will be a coming to maturity to stop seeking to defend moral principles with abstract rationality, and a great advance at last to take Hume's moral theory seriously (1739, 1751). If, as he argues, justice is an artificial virtue, we should study systematically the social conventions by which it is constructed.

The most interesting attempt to develop a moral theory based on risk is Charles Fried's *Anatomy of Values* (1970). He elaborates a general Kantian framework of respect for individual rights so as to include a time span within which each individual is assumed to be working out his own life's moral project. Considering what kind of individual he plans to be, what rational consistency he tries to put into his life plan, what risks he knows he must take to achieve it, and especially incorporating the certain expectation of his own death at the end of it, the individual has a private risk budget. In his interactions with others, he reckons upon a common risk pool into which each dips when his own behavior exposes others to dangers. Any society operates its rules of mutual accountability, judgment, and retribution from the principle of whether the individual is trying to draw out more rights to expose others to risk than he is prepared to accept as drafts upon his own risk budget. The risk pool is a brilliant innovation for putting risk and moral philosophy into a frame of discourse that is sociologically rich. It also suggests how the discussion of risk aversion could include an assessment of the social probabilities in the same analysis along with assessment of the physical probabilities of risk. Instead of asking how much risk is acceptable to you, the general question would be what kind of society do you

14

want? The risk issue could be more elaborately discriminated between kinds of risks and categories of persons at risk if the particular kind of society could be specified, and if it could be recognized that each type of society has its custom-built ethical system.

Cost-benefit analysis would give very different results if applied within different ethical systems. An ingenious attempt to work out the ethical foundations of cost-benefit analysis defines four ethical systems with enough rigor to permit formal quantitative analysis (Ben-David et al. 1979; Schulze and Kneeze 1981). A utilitarian philosophy requires "the greatest good of the greatest number." Translated to a social decision rule, this requires the government to act so as to maximize the utility of society as a whole. An egalitarian system holds that the well-being of society is measured by the well-being of the worst-off person in that society, a notion that would lead to a totally egaliltarian distribution of utility (Rawls 1971). This criterion would emphasize equality based on need. A totally elitist system measures the well-being of society by the well-being of the best-off individual. The concept of merit can be elitist and economic productivity can be used as a criterion to rationalize a defined elite.

> The gasoline shortage of the summer of 1979 moved Senator Hayakawa of California to comment, "The important thing is that a lot of the poor don't need gas because they are not working." . . . Obviously it will be better to keep B alive to serve A, i.e. to contribute to his well-being. . . . Thus subsistence is typically required for B . . . . Similarly, if we have two succeeding generations, it may well be "best" for the first generation to save as much as possible to make the next generation better off. This attitude has been manifest among many immigrants to the United States with respect to their children. [Schulze and Kneeze 1981]

Lastly, the libertarian ethical system is an amalgam embodied in the principle that individual freedoms prevail except where others may be harmed (see Nozick 1974). A basic distinction between these types lines up those who emphasize individual rights (egalitarianism, libertarianism) and those who emphasize the good of the whole (utilitarian philosophy and elitism).

If any one doubts whether espousing one or other of these ethical teachings depends heavily on the strength of group commitments and degree of social differentiation let them read Gerald

Mars's *Cheats at Work* (1982). In this analysis of occupational crime, the opportunities for illicit gains are precisely wrapped into the description of each occupational niche. For example, occupations in which an interdependent team is internally differentiated will be prone to what Mars calls "wolf pack" forms of cheating. Woe betide the unhappy patient in such a nursing home or guest in such a hotel—he will be thoroughly victimized by the elitist philosophers (from bellboy and bartender to chambermaids and maître d'hôtel) who run in the well-ordered pack. When the organization of the work leaves the individual free to serve his own self-interests, unsupervised, beware of "hawk" crimes, such as the switching of supplies from the intended destination to one where the opportunist sees more profit. In each case the standardized and shared moral perceptions of the workers are shown to respond closely to a rational calculation of individual self-interest within the structure of possible initiatives.

It is astonishing how rare in the social science literature are analyses of these kinds which seek a systematic view of the relation between ethical principles and the social environment. Another innovative approach to the subject is William Torry's analysis of the shift in ideas of distributive justice that occurs between normal times and prolonged crises such as famine (1982). Now that we are becoming aware of our implication in each other's perception of risks, there is some urgency in trying to know the association between a given ethical system and the social order that it supports. When you choose your big risks it will be as well to choose your fellow crew and passengers and to have a say in how the lifeboat will be organized.

Probability has by no means yet claimed its full domain in twentieth-century thought. At present, probability analysis, though heavily used, plays only an ancillary role: It is treated as a robot-like servant of the social sciences. It provides a method of solving problems by assembling and analyzing the data. It does not yet set the limits of questions or select them as it does in the physical sciences. But it is gradually asserting its own independent basis of authority. These once-separate items of danger now treated together as risk will not disintegrate into separate elements. Instead, a new understanding of risk perception will supply a theoretical frame for mainstream sociological thought. To see what such a new encompassing structure might be like calls for backtracking into the history of philosophy and probability theory. Hacking (1975) says that the alchemists

> believed that the world worked according to its primary qualities, but that they could only experiment on the secondary qualities. There was still the belief that there were true, necessary connections among the primary qualities that made everything go. If I may be forgiven the crudeness in such a brief sketch, Boyle, for the first time succeeding in getting behind the phenomena, found no scholastic causes . . . necessary connections were nowhere in sight . . . where we had hoped for causes and rational demonstrations, we found only constant conjunctions and lawlike regularity. [pp. 182–83]

Risk perception studies are still at the stage of looking for causes. Though the seventeenth century quickly saw the physical sciences adopt the new mode of discourse, philosophy lagged behind. Descartes was still aiming to make the world safe for such as Galileo and himself by developing independent a priori foundations of knowledge. He came on the scene too quickly; a little later, with so much scientific knowledge founded on probability, "Hume has become possible" (Foucault 1970). But the study of social behavior is still not brought squarely under this aegis. Hume proposed a probabilistic approach to both moral judgment and perception of natural phenomena. The methodological problems inherent in the topic of risk acceptability may force the so-called social sciences to make themselves at home in this part of the twentieth century.

Probability theory will eventually transform the assumptions about rational behavior that currently guide research about risk perception. The probabilities at issue will include the expectations of the rational agent about the probable reactions of his fellow rational agents and also the probability of such expectations being transformed into steady conventions with agreed forms of signaling. In other words, a systematic cultural dimension will emerge from the probabilizing of attitudes and the probabilizing of the hierarchy of moral values adopted by different rational agents according to the different social environments they are working to build. This is a more fundamental way of posing the central problem of democracy than to treat it as merely one of differences of opinion or tastes which might arise from personal happenstance. Michael Thompson (1982, 1983) has analyzed moral attitudes to risks from energy and shown them to arise from different social (and therefore cultural) experiences within the same community. He has suggested how, if the variations could be recognized as legitimate, they could be made the basis of flexibly adjusted local policies. The structure of society and its moral basis will be part of the probabilistic analysis.

The wrong way to think of the social factors that influence risk perception is to treat them as smudges which blur a telescope lens and distort the true image. This metaphor justifies a negative approach. But the social point of view thus dismissed includes moral judgments about the kind of society in which we want to live. Why should they be summarily brushed aside? A better kind of analysis might treat such transformations of the image not as distortions but as improvements: the result of a sharper focus that assesses the society along with its assessments of risks.

Chapter 2 The Emergence of a New Subdiscipline

Summary: This chapter introduces the public concern about risk from technology which encouraged different disciplines to converge upon the subject of public tolerance of risks. It traces the origins of the new subdiscipline.

Historians and philosophers of science are interested in the origins of distinctive sets of ideas. The subdiscipline of risk perception affords an interesting contemporary case. Its emergence can reasonably be dated to 1969 when Chauncey Starr's article "Social Benefit Versus Technological Risk" in *Science* provoked controversy. The controversy gave rise to conferences, the conferences gave rise to research institutes and journals. These quickly gave rise to a new profession and to a considerable literature. The new subdiscipline is not only a defined historical entity. Its restrictive assumptions and preferred methods provide it with structure and reinforce its internal channels of communication. Like any other discipline it is equipped with screening devices which exclude methods or information incompatible with the knowledge which it has already processed.

In the 1950s the nuclear community and electrical industries expected to be thanked for creating new energy sources which would ensure productivity, wealth, and health for the world. Gradually, through the 1960s they were the target of increasingly articulate, hostile public criticism. Government, recognizing its

19

policy dilemmas, and industry, trying to justify itself, asked what could be known about public attitudes to risk.

Risk Definitions

The definition of risk has naturally been at issue as the special disciplines studying risk perception develop. The United Nations recommends two divergent definitions for evaluating toxicity in chemicals: (a) focused on properties of pure probability; (b) focused on properties of utility.

(a) "Risk is a statistical concept and has been defined by the preparatory committee of the United Nations Conference on the Human Environments as the expected frequency of undesirable effects arising from exposure to a pollutant" (World Health Organization, 1978:19). No attempt to define the degree of harm is included here.

(b) "Most literature on this subject begins with the thesis that risk (R) can be estimated as some sort of product of the probability (P) of the event times the severity of the harm (H), or $R = P \times H$" (Campbell 1980). Benefits enter this equation because it treats safety as a measure of the acceptability of some degree of risk. The two definitions have different policy implications. By concentrating only on probable frequencies of bad outcomes, the first definition gives the policymaker no headaches about how to compare harms with benefits, and some would claim it wisely steers clear of the scientific pretensions of utility calculations. Interestingly the idea that risk means only probabilities of harm is very widespread, even where "risk-benefit" is a method deliberately compared with cost-benefit analysis.

What does reasonable riskiness mean? What are acceptable levels of risk? Is the American public risk-averse? How does this new image of risk aversion fit with the favorite old image of the American way of life—entrepreneurs made rich by risk-taking? Does the lay public perceive risks differently from the experts and if there is discrepancy, how can it be reduced? How new is the confrontation of brutal industrialists and a fearful public? The questions echo Blake's inveighing against cruel nineteenth-century mill owners. If that perspective gives the right analogy, strict regulation would surely be in order. But regulation is costly. So are safety precautions. Then the issue broadens out to allocating the costs of safe production and from there to the general merits and demerits of economic growth. Industrial development never eliminates dangers to life and limb; excluding one source of danger introduces another: Asbestos was originally a great discovery for checking fire damage; lead was a means of providing steady water supplies. Perhaps the right solution was to refuse economic growth. If only the nation were of one mind, the government's task would be clearer: Education of the public must narrow the disagreement. Early polls show that the blue-collar workers are mainly in favor of nuclear power for peaceful purposes. Does this indicate that they should be educated away from their short-sighted views by a paternalistic government? The official labor movement in America is divided on the issue. The people who are worried about the environment were first seen as a middle-class elite interested in preserving their mountain holidays or as rural folk interested in their own backyards.

Public Awareness of Risks

Considerable polling and other research documents this topic, but the results tend to be inconclusive. The most consistent reviews come from Mitchell's surveys conducted for the Resources for the Future (1979). In 1974–76 the pro-environment lobby was thought to be slightly differentiated from the rest of the population in being younger, with higher income and education levels and higher status occupations. The members of the pro-environment organizations (a very small proportion of the general public) showed these distinctions much more than the larger group of pro-environment sympathizers (Mitchell 1979, 1980b; Logan and Nelkin 1980). Among supporters of the Anti-Nuclear Power Movement, women were more committed than men (Nelkin 1981a, 1981b). The New York *Times*/CBS Poll of 1981 found the pro-environment movement had the following characteristics: young, urban dwellers and people living on the east and west coasts. It did not find that income, education, race, party identification, or ideological position affected support for environmental policies significantly.

Several investigators have remarked on the limitations of public knowledge of risks (Kunreuther et al. 1978), that individuals erratically overestimate some and underestimate other categories of risk (Harvey 1979), that the public tends to overestimate dangers of rare events and underestimate those of common events (Slovic, Fischhoff, and Lichtenstein 1979a, 1981), that in familiar contexts the private individual makes a closely approximate estimate of actual risks (Green 1980; Green and Brown 1981a), that individuals tend to be optimistic about probabilities affected by their own behavior (Lalonde 1974).

21

Through the 1960s the movement of criticism spreads and gains wide national support against nuclear and chemical wastes, against inadequately protected asbestos workers, and against air and water pollution. Parallel movements appear in Europe and Japan. But in the United States it is so successful that it succeeds in stopping the development of nuclear power. Kasperson (1980) wrote, "The futures of nuclear energy are at a critical juncture. If a socially acceptable and implementable solution to the radioactive waste problem is not found within the next several years, the growth of nuclear energy as a source of power production will probably come to a halt in the U.S. and in numerous other countries." Alvin Weinberg (1982), in defense of what he regards as an industry at risk, proposes research and education to prepare for a second nuclear era, assuming that the first era is now closed in the United States, Sweden, Austria, Norway, and Denmark. However, in other places the industry thrives.

The bewildered nuclear community wants to know why they have become so unpopular. For them the problem is one of a tragic difference between an exaggerated public perception of the actual dangers at issue and the scientific facts. For the not indifferent public, there is a different tragic discrepancy, in which safety has been exaggerated by the other side. The new subdiscipline of risk perception emerges in response to these important concerns. It is constituted by three different disciplines: (1) there is the *engineering approach,* extended from the analysis of risk to the analysis of perception; (2) there is the *ecological approach;* (3) there is the *cognitive science approach.* Theoretically sophisticated, but naive in social thought, each discipline transferred only a small part of its traditional methods to the new field.

(1) The engineering contribution assumes that the public consists of isolated independent individuals who naturally behave like engineers: They want to know the facts and these facts, once clearly presented, will convince them of the safety or riskiness of a proposal. The public is to be told what its normal load of risk is, in crossing a street or driving a car in everyday life, and how much extra load of risk it will carry if a nuclear power station is placed in the vicinity. The risk is sometimes calculated in days or minutes taken off the normal expectation of life, or in fraction percentages of several million parts, illustrated with graphs. Understanding will lay fear to rest.

The engineers felt impatient with the social sciences. The methods used in technology for risk identification and assessment could surely be extended to questions of social acceptability (Starr 1969; Farmer 1981). Risk-benefit was a method for interpreting contemporary consensus on social values. Starr, taking the term "revealed preference" from economics and tracing the present distribution of risks across many activities, purported to show that what is tolerated can be regarded as a tolerable distribution. His first exercise produced some interesting concepts: (1) the concept of *limits of acceptability*: Risk acceptability increases with increase in benefits within certain ranges; (2) *natural levels* of risks: Risks below the natural hazards level seem to be ignored by the public; (3) risks taken *voluntarily* may be tolerated far in excess of the natural level from disease, but rarely those taken involuntarily; (4) the distinction between *chronic* and *catastrophic* risks. This seminal article, which set the initial terms of the discussion of risk perception, raised controversy about how the data sustained the statistical analyses. Much was also said about whether knowing how the death rate from one technology compares with natural levels of hazard would influence public attitudes. To many persons, statements such that "the annual risk from living near a nuclear power plant is equivalent to the risk of riding an extra three miles in an automobile" appear ludicrous because they fail to give adequate consideration to the important differences in the nature of the risks from these two technologies (Slovic, Fischhoff, and Lichtenstein 1981). Little is said (Green 1980) about whether the abstract composite concept of "risks" ever enters into individual thinking about risk-taking: nor about the uneven distribution of risks over social categories. Starr is convinced that it is important not to let the will of the majority be overridden by minorities. For a fair review of Starr see Slovic, Fischhoff, and Lichtenstein 1979b.

That quantified methods of risk assessment are highly manipulable is so well understood that they do not carry the authority and objective weight that their users intend. So OSHA took a hard and fast line against risk quantification (at least for carcinogens in the work place) in the deliberations of the Interagency Regulatory Liaison Group's Panel on risk assessment (Carter 1979). Anyone who has read Self (1975) on the fantasies involved in assessing the value of a Norman church in the elaborate cost-benefit analysis employed by the Roskill Commission on the siting of the third London Airport will understand why CBA applied to large social issues fell into grave disrepute in England since 1970. Criticisms of Starr's approach is a unifying theme for early risk-perception studies (Kates 1977:5; Otway and Cohen 1975; Slovic, Fischhoff, and Lichtenstein 1979b, 1981).

The result has not allayed public fears. It has provoked a lively set of reproaches against the irrelevance and inexactitude of such measures.

To get a feel for the mystification and the furor, read Inhaber's report (1978) to the Canadian Atomic Energy Control Board and his article in *Science* (1979), in which he argued that nuclear is safer than conventional energy sources. "Inhaber's report is a morass of mistakes, including double counting, highly selective use (and misuse) of data, untenable assumptions, inconsistencies in the treatment of different technologies, and conceptual confusions . . . correcting just his largest errors completely transforms his results, raising the upper limits of nuclear risks to the public and occupational health into the lower part of the uncertainty range for coal and oil, and dropping the health risks of the non-conventional sources into the middle of the uncertainty range for nuclear . . . by propagating an analysis riddled with distortions, errors, and inconsistencies, Inhaber has muddied rather than illuminated even the circumscribed part of the risk problem he tackled" (Holdren et al. 1979). In Britain, Sir John Hill, chairman of the Atomic Energy Authority, had declared in 1976 that the debate on nuclear energy, was largely about "non-problems. . . the public debate of science fiction" (Williams 1980:273). The credibility of expert risk judgments is in doubt: "Central to public risk assessment is suspicion about industry, utility and regulator commitment to reduce and minimize these risks" (Kasperson et al. 1980).

(2) The ecological research starts with the work of White (1952) on flood disasters. A steady flow of criticism of theory and analysis of risk situations has been maintained (Burton et al. 1978; Fischhoff et al. 1978), particularly by the Center for Technology, Environment and Development at Clark University. Its thought-provoking publications, and especially the journal *Environment*, have discussed many central issues of fact, interpretation, and ethics and have raised the level of public debate on risk from technology. Where risk perception is concerned the theoretical basis of this approach is not highly developed except for an ecological model of risk response (Kates 1977, 1978). According to this sequential model, different sectors of the public (like communities of plants and insects) go through the stages of a developing life cycle, sequentially encountering and adapting to various hazards. This approach is careful to distinguish the term hazard from risk. Indeed, the shift of terminology helps to bridge the difference between plant ecology and human ecology, for the living elements in the former can be said to react to hazards, whereas they do not act (by definition) as rational agents calculating risks. Furthermore, reasonably enough, the assessment of combined probabilities of an occurrence and the magnitude of

its consequences is too specialized a form of calculation to be helpful in thinking of the ordinary person's perceptions. In this approach inputs of information or experience are traced to outputs of changed opinions. Epidemiological models of contact with information and developmental models of experience with hazards are worked out. Hazards have been sorted and classified according to their perceived characteristics. Variations in public response to dramatic or minor events, such as sudden disasters killing a few hundred people or long, slow, disastrous processes with casualties mounting by hundreds of thousands over the years, produce different profiles of the risk characteristics of events and allow for comparisons between perceived and actual hazards.

Criticism of Ecological Approach

Torry (1979b) argues that so-called human ecology has paid scant attention to the humans. In his review of *The Environment as Hazard* (Burton, Kates, and White 1978), Torry has many hard criticisms of the book as a whole. Of White's interview protocols, which hold culture and social organization constant, he says: "Yet, what individuals do or what they say they do about protecting the security of their world depends on a large number of factors which would include their social status, level of cultural literacy, access to credit sources such as those embedded in kinship networks, technical expertise, size and diversity of assets, employment options, household labour requirements, membership in voluntary organizations, productive capacity of capital, and commitment to cultural values and religious conventions. As such, culture-bound categories do not enter into the survey design, the units of analysis turn out to be mere collections of individuals rather than samples of societies . . . accordingly, 'denying risks,' 'reducing risks' or any of a number of other rubrics by which the findings in these sections are organized, represent nothing more than crude glosses . . . labels do not constitute explanations and contribute little to an understanding of individual adjustment processes. One wants to know, for instance, how coping options depend upon individual social rank, popularity, marital status, character attributes, wealth and intelligence: how these factors correlate and why their composition weight varies from one society to the next, or with respect to different hazard types . . . that community institutions and values decisively govern human vulnerability to natural disturbances and that they articulate the individual and national adjustments, is axiomatic."

In the ecological approach, hazard is taken as the independent variable and people's response to it as dependent. The parallel between plants and humans weakens if the concept of hazard is recognized as dependent. The people whose perception is being studied are living in a world constructed from their own concepts: These include the concept of what is hazardous.

Anthropologists writing of tribal cultures are forced to make a clear distinction between the analysts' model and the actors' model of what is happening. The actors' model covers only the tribal theory about the world. The investigator who stands outside the tribal culture observes how the actors draw a line between consequences and causes. Comparing these lines in different cultures exposes the bias of the actors' model.

Risk-Aversion from Inside the Actors' Model of the World

Working only within the actors' model imparts cultural bias, as two important, early surveys of risk acceptability show (Lowrance 1976; Rowe 1977). In spite of his title, *Of Acceptable Risk,* Lowrance says little about the issue of what makes risk acceptable and he also treats risk probabilities as objective. Rowe gives the list of factors influencing perception of risk (practically standard since Starr 1969), differentiating between victim's and benefitter's views, between expectancies of control, voluntary and involuntary subjection to risk, effects on perception of magnitude and visibility of types of risk. He does not recognize that if culture were admitted as a variable one could not say that human society is generally risk aversive because many cultures demand risk-seeking. Rowe implies that the line between natural and man-made disaster is unproblematic (p. 158). Philip Schrodt (1980) has argued that policymakers and numerous social scientists show a cultural bias toward assuming risk aversion to be general, a bias explained by (a) the use of worst-plausible-case evaluation of risk and benefit, (b) the marginal evaluation of risks and benefits, (c) the use of the current distinction between voluntary and involuntary risks and (d) the discounting of future benefits.

To define hazards as "recognized causes of death or loss," whether technological or natural, is to stay within a cultural definition of causes. This leaves no scope for considering perception here, except normatively as something that could be improved upon, and all the emphasis falls upon the difference between natural and other causes.

Natural Causes

The line between natural and man-made causes is always drawn in a social process of allocating responsibility. Consequently, it is a wavy, unsteady line, always in debate and reflecting current cultural bias. Chief Justice Rose Elizabeth Bird recently protested that the "distinction between artificial and natural conditions should be rejected . . . there is an inherent injustice" in a rule that permits landowners to escape all liability "merely by allowing nature to take its course." In this case a company that owned land in Malibu disclaimed responsibility when a landslide destroyed a home, on the grounds that they could not be made responsible for all natural disasters (Los Angeles *Times*, December 21, 1981). "Just as notions of *Acts of God* and *Acts of Man* coalesce, so do these distinctions between intention, accident and incident" (Kates 1977:56). Burton, Kates, and White (1978) have always maintained that "hazards are by definition human phenomena." Likewise Fischhoff et al. (1978), but it is easier to say this than to take it into account in the ensuing analysis.

Even the definition of hazard as inability to cope still stands within the actors' model. But at least this definition connects physical causes and physical consequences with the coping capability of a rational subject. This is closer to a theory of perception since it allows that expectations about coping create the quality of hazardousness, and a theory of perception is necessary for thinking about risk acceptability.

Coping

The emphasis on ability to cope goes along with a different set of assumptions about risk management. Instead of assuming general risk reduction as the ideal, Clark assumes that effective hazard management must seek to increase ability to tolerate error and so to improve ability to take productive risks (Clark 1977). Turning the focus back to coping abilities would help to understand the sociological and cultural aspects of risk perception.

It seems very plausible that the primary concern of the perceiving subject be whether coping is feasible, difficult, or impossible. There is no perception until information is coded for interpretation by matching perceptors. Economists often speak of information as if it was an active agent flowing, making an impact, getting lost, or stopped by blocks in its path, a possession which some have and others lack. These habits of speech echo an eighteenth century theory of perception according to which sense impressions strike the mind of the perceiver as a bright light strikes the retina of the eye. Whereas information does not even become information at all unless it is somehow seen and coded by the perceiver.

(3) Cognitive science has tended to dominate risk perception,

extending its assumptions and psychometric methods to the whole scene. This means that from a technical point of view the most sophisticated work in the subdiscipline is found under the general aegis of the theory of rational behavior, accepting its axioms and restrictive assumptions (see chapter 4). Though initially the different kinds of work appeared with different sets of named authors, there has been an increasing tendency for them to converge, the seminal pieces being co-authored by experts from several backgrounds.

When an established discipline applies itself to a new field, something inevitably happens to its methods: Sometimes a rule of thumb is transferred, sometimes only a metaphor. The engineers made a bold leap when they applied their regular working method to public acceptance of risk. Most of their problems of analysis follow from not being sufficiently aware of shifts of metaphor. The "tolerance" of physical strain by a machine means something different from human tolerance of insults or adversities; likewise, the ideas of "risk load" and "strain." But their exercise is not a mere rhetorical façade, since it remains faithful to the normal practices of engineering where tolerance is revealed as not breaking down. They are making no difference in method whether they are aggregating the strains that a bridge or a human system reveals that it can bear. But they are not making a lot of sense, for reasons which will be reiterated in the following pages.

By contrast, the biologists who moved over to risk perception had the opposite difficulty, having left most of their theoretical equipment behind. What can an ecologist do without an ecosystem and what is an ecosystem without resource constraints? These biologists use a crude notion of perception, as if it were a matter of seeing what risks are there, instead of a matter of selecting a pattern out of what is there. The pattern's properties do not force themselves on the perceiver's eye. So the important issues of risk perception can never be analyzed with an inventory of the physical features of events, their scale of damage, suddenness, or duration.

Cognitive science will be considered in chapters 3 and 4. The idea of rationality must dominate the study of risk perception. The idea of the rational, risk-perceiving agent is built up (must be built up?) on the model of the rational investigator. Both are driven to seek order in the world; both recognize inconsistency; both assess probability.

Chapter 3   Perception of Risk

Summary: This chapter compares the treatment of perception in humans and animals. Animal psychologists assume that the emotional responses which alert attention, sustain or divert it, contribute positively to the functioning of the organism and to the survival of the species. Human psychology tries to separate habits and emotions (such as fear or excitement) from the testing of cognition. In such tests, humans tend to perform in ways that call the basic concepts of rationality into question. Research then focuses upon the inadequacy of the human perceptual apparatus, upon dysfunction. The social processes involved in concept formation need to be systematically included in studies of public risk perception.

The best established results of risk research show that individuals have a strong but unjustified sense of subjective immunity. In very familiar activities there is a tendency to mimimize the probability of bad outcomes. Apparently, people underestimate risks which are supposed to be under their control. They reckon they can cope with familiar situations. They also underestimate risks of events which are rarely expected to happen. Our first question about perception of risk is why so many, in their layman's role, judge everyday hazards to be safe and think themselves able to cope when the event shows they cannot.

Subjective Immunity

The experience of the National Commission on Product Safety finds the consumer ready to opt for a slight saving in price rather than for cheaply bought increase in safety. Familiarity seems to breed confidence in farmers living on flood plains (White 1952) and in smokers, pedestrians in traffic, and drivers; those living near nuclear plants are less anxious about radiation than others (Guedeney and Mendel 1973); engineers and mechanics tend to be

29

overconfident in their own technology (Slovic, Fischhoff, and Lichtenstein 1981). In some high-risk occupations, confidence and familiarity are enhanced by benefits (Lee 1981). However, familiarity often works the other way (Slovic, Fischhoff, and Lichtenstein 1980).

Most common everyday dangers tend to be ignored. On the other end of the scale of probabilities, the most infrequent, low-probability dangers also tend to be played down. Putting these tendencies together, the individual seems to cut off his perceptions of highly probable risks so that his immediate world seems to be safer than it is and, as he also cuts off his interest in low-probability events, distant dangers also fade. For a species well adapted to survive, neglecting low-frequency events seems an eminently reasonable strategy. To attend equally to all the low probabilities of disaster would diffuse attention and even produce a dangerous lack of focus. From the point of view of species survival, the sense of subjective immunity is also adaptive if it allows humans to keep cool in the midst of dangers, to dare to experiment, not to be thrown off balance by evidence of failures. Here is surely one of the interesting differences between human and animal psychology. Perhaps some of the problems about the evolution of social behavior could be broken down into testable propositions about the social sources of confidence and the felicitous effects for the human race of over-confidence (Trivers 1972).

Put to the test formally humans do not seem to be good at rational thinking. They also have weak and erratic memory.

Memory Research

Memory research relies heavily on language, while much of human remembering and cognition is independent of speech. Significantly, attempts to establish parallels to human amnesia in animal laboratory experiments largely fail; Nadel (1980) suggests that this may be because human memory relates to language in a special way. Some part of human response to hazards will be rooted in our animal nature. This will be one reason why the psychological knowledge of human risk perception is in an elementary stage. Furthermore, studies of human memory suggest that we cannot approach human cognition by studying weakness of memory. Elizabeth Loftus's book *Memory* (1980) says much more about why we forget than how we remember. The latter seems to be distinctly haphazard.

Since in the case of human memory what is stored and retrievable depends on control of attention, and since attention depends on social signals and social pressures, the case stands for turning the problem the right way up and focusing on the individual's coding of social experience.

The psychologists recommend to those who know what the risks really are to concentrate on better communication with the lay public. Normally wise advice, in this case education about risks has not got a very encouraging record.

Weakness of Education

A chorus of agreement on how little can be achieved by public education for better risk perception is heard from such authorities as Roder (1961), and Nelkin (1974) who describes the massive Swedish campaign to educate the public about nuclear power and other energy sources. Slovic, Lichtenstein, and Fischhoff (1974), writing with special reference to the problem of nuclear risk, state: "Our own view is that educational attempts designed to reduce the 'perception gap' are probably doomed to failure." Later, Slovic, Fischhoff, and Lichtenstein (1981) comment that "many people's mental images of a nuclear accident include the spectre of hundreds of thousands, even millions, of immediate deaths accompanied by incalculable and irreversible damage to the environment. These images bear little resemblance to the views of industry officials (and most technical experts). . . . Industry proponents have tended to attribute this perception gap to public ignorance and irrationality. We question this attitude and we doubt that its proposed remedy, education, will succeed" (p. 33).

But this chorus is matched by another (sometimes including the same voices) recommending that more effort be made to improve public understanding by better educational campaigns. Joining the second chorus are Kunreuther et al. (1978). "Existing evidence regarding the extent to which media publicity, films or graphic displays have generated concern with future disasters is not very reassuring," Kunreuther and his coauthors write (p. 251), adding, "If governmental aid is deemed desirable, a concerted effort should be made to disseminate information to the affected population" (p. 254). In research undertaken for the Fire Research Station, Green and Brown (1981) first clarified what is understood by the term "risk"; they then found that where sufficiently reliable and precise objective estimates are available, their respondents' beliefs are quite accurate. It seems people first take a moral position—what ought to exist—and couple this with pragmatic considerations looking toward a complex future; in this light it makes sense to recommend that more and better information be given.

The faith in education is a logical next step from the initial acceptance of risk perception as a problem of misperceptions by the lay public. Such an approach leads to the alternative recommendation of closer regulatory control or for more psychological research on failures of communication. Labeling theory focuses on how the mode of presentation affects evaluation. The conference reported by Morris et al. (1980) gives an overview of labeling theory applied to perception of risks, dealing with whether direct regulation, free market forces, or compulsory labeling (a form of regulation) work best for the different health risks. Kasperson et al. (1980) give a critical summary of the arguments for and against public education about nuclear energy.

Disappointment with the difficulty of educating the general public supports another trend that came near to calling us all irrational. Jonathan Cohen (1981) argues that the conditions for rationality are so flexible that by invoking the full arrray of motives and goals to which an individual subscribes, any decision can be exempted from the charge of irrationality. The argument essentially expects rational thought to be exercised through two kinds of competence, one a universal pan-human competence in logical operations (avoiding contradiction and expecting coherence) and the other a culturally acquired competence in recognizing, assembling, and sorting particular elements. Cohen dubs the combination "intuition" and argues that since the input from culture can never be determined, there is no way of proving any choice or decision to be irrational.

Before this rather weak vindication of our rationality, risk perception had already tempered its terminology, claiming that individuals are not irrational, just weak in probabilistic thinking. But when we look at what understanding probabilism requires, it does not sound so difficult. Apparently, we need to grasp only three principles: randomness, statistical independence, and sampling variability (Hogarth 1980, chap. 2). Furthermore, when we consider any technical activity whatever, we find that any of us, without regard to schooling, is capable of using all three principles. Hunters, fishers, farmers, and sailors use their grasp of probabilism to assess their materials, the predicted behavior of fish or sheep, or tides or weather. They know all about random variation in the accuracy of their instruments, they disregard inferences from too small sample size, and without knowing statistics they know a lot about the practical equivalent of statistical independence. If they did not, they would not survive long as craftsmen or navigators, and so forth. What is difficult is not the informal practice of probabilistic thinking in a familiar context, but formal probability analysis.

The whole discussion of human capability to think probabilistic-ally has an uncomfortable similarity to the turn-of-the-century dis-cussion of primitive mentality (Wynne 1982[a]; Lévy Bruhl 1966). The natives in the colonial territories seemed to have a perverse and unreliable grasp of logic: Enlightened administrators tried to understand their intellectual weakness by studying anthropology. Brian Wynne turns the analogy the other way round when he de-rides claims made in the name of scientific rationality: "the percep-tion of criticism as a threat to the whole way of thought is charac-teristic of primitive societies which have an insulated and homogeneous experience. There appear to be no intrinsic discon-tinuities between scientific and primitive thought; the differences lie in some important social characteristics" (1982b:168). In partic-ular, Wynne attributes intellectual rigidity to social insulation.

Since scientists who explicitly use probability theory also fail in these tests that floor less formally trained subjects, we need to look more closely at the questions in the psychology experiments. It turns out that they all relate to a particular field of expertise, that of probability theory as such (Krantz et al. 1983). Experi-mental research comparing subjects with different amounts of formal training showed how intuitive versions of the law of large numbers are used as a heuristic. Formal training increased the frequency and quality of its use.

In other words, the culturally learned intuitions which guide our judgment for any of our fields of competence teach us enough probabilistic principles but they are heavily culture-bound. We are all lost when we venture beyond the scope of our culturally given intuitions. Presumably the technically competent probabilist would be equally lost if asked to predict outside his skilled experience, though he would be good at formally structur-ing the problem.

Though this may save humans from the academic charge of not being capable of thinking probabilistically, it leaves several practical problems for risk perception. Particularly, it enhances the gap between the expert's and the lay person's judgment. If people can only think probabilistically from a position of expert competence, and if there is no way for all or many of us to be-come experts in modern weaponry or nuclear power, the question of how we are to make a political judgment of such risks is still open. This story starts out with a need to understand why experts in industry and government cannot convince the public of the safety of new technology. The generalized tendency of humans turns out to be quite the other way, not naturally timorous but rather overintrepid and difficult to persuade of the reality of dangers. But if the dangers in question are thought to be inflicted by a powerful minority (the industrialists) on a helpless majority, the sense of subjective immunity is not evoked. The difference is that the attitude to risks inflicted by others is political. The public considering new technology may not necessarily be afraid so much as angry. Risk perception may not be the issue at all, but indignation at bamboozlement and exploitation. If so, we need to understand attitudes to blame.

Attribution theory purports to give a wide framework for considering how blame is laid.

Attribution Theory

For a summary, see Heider (1958). Studies informed by attribution theory have identified a sense of a locus of control, and a sense of helplessness in responses to stress. Risk perception and stress studies overlap because of the finding that a generalized expectation of being in control reduces the experience of stress (Jones and Davis 1961; Rotter 1966). The approach parallels the interest in risk perception studies in subjects who perceive their risks to be involuntarily assumed. The collection of essays edited by Hamilton and Warburton (1979) emphasizes the more clearly cognitive sources of coping with strain (see "Coping" in chapter 2). However, the main sources of social support and confidence are here found exclusively in early childhood and family bonds. A rare attempt (Brown et al. 1975) to relate stress to a wider, adult social context drops the cognitive emphasis.

First there is the judgment as to causes, whether natural or human. If the damage is man-made, the attribution of responsibility and blame goes to the locus of control. There is a choice of acknowledging our own fault, pinning blame on another, deciding whether the other was informed and motivated to do harm. If we are already hostile to the presumed agent of harm, our blaming tends to be stronger, and if we suspect the agent of benefiting from our loss, the adverse judgment is even stronger. Although psychologists find that people differ in the extent to which they take or give blame or exonerate, they are professionally biased toward looking into personality structure to explain differences. Attribution theory pays little attention to the social training which selects and reinforces particular blaming attitudes.

34

But this is readily understood. No guidelines are yet established about how to take the values generated in the social environment systematically into account.

When we turn to research into values we find that either it uses standard administrative categories for anchoring expressed values to segments of society or it avoids tracing expectations about risks to any socially defined categories.

Psychologists are beginning to recognize this problem. Jaspers (1981) argues that the social nature of attitudes has been so completely overlooked that manifestly social responses are treated as individual dispositions. Referring to his own earlier work on cognitive and emotional differentiation, "One needs a truly social point of view to realize that what appears to be a process of individual differentiation increasing with children's age is in effect the emergence of a shared response hierarchy requiring a social explanation." Further methodological weaknesses flowing from the same difficulty are analyzed in Gergen and Gergen (1973, 1982). To come out of arduous survey research with clusters of expectation which rest upon each other is interesting (Mitchell 1980a, 1980b), but some exit from the data to the theory of risk perception would be better still.

Value Syndromes

Several scholars have tried to examine the bunching of attitudes together in terms of their incompatibilities and affinities. Spangler (1980, 1981) develops the concept of syndrome; "a set of concurrent concepts including related emotions and decision predispositions that form an identifiable attitudinal pattern." Syndromes have a collective character, involving moral ideas of good and bad and reflecting shared social experience. Syndromes are characterized by the beliefs they select and by the interrelated dialectic considerations they ignore. This is one of the rare cases where risk perception research is interested in selective attention. But it does not take the next step of considering how social alignments act as focusing factors. Heberlein and Black (1981) attempt to identify "behavior molecules," norms, beliefs, social support and structural variables, recognizing the complexity of normative structures in modern society. Other research in progress attempts to relate values to social and cognitive strategies. For example, Stallen and Tomas (1981) are developing a survey for identifying four responses to technological threat (the secure, the defensive, the vigilant, and the adaptive). Evidently, there will soon be greater confidence and sophistication in dealing with the interface be-

tween the individual's perceptions and public attitudes (Back and
Gergen 1963).

Our knowledge of risk perception is controlled by the choice of
methods.

Fundamental Methodology

Many concerns have been voiced about methodological problems, most of them common to all attempts to identify public attitudes and values and not specially peculiar to risk perception.
Thomas draws attention to intractable problems of aggregation
(1981), Green and Brown to the results being artifacts of scales
supplied in the questionnaires (1980). No one voices such sweep-
ing criticisms as Plott (1978), who discusses risk policy issues as
examples of grave, unsolved problems underlying contemporary social theory. (1) One problem arises from the effects of ordering answers to risk-benefit choice questions in different ways: At the individual level of analysis, one can get absolutely inconsistent
measurement, "depending upon a subtle and innocent-looking aspect of the measurement system"; (2) Group attitudes and group
choices do not follow the same laws as individual choice; (3) Group
choice itself is sensitive to decision-making or agenda-setting procedures. Conclusion: Much theory and philosophy evolving from
these efforts suggests that the concept of group preference itself is
the source of error. It seems to involve the classic fallacy of composition by assuming that a property of the individual, a preference,
is also a property of the group. The application of risk-benefit analysis rests squarely on the concept of group preference as a founda-
tional property. This is a rare discussion of the implications of Arrow's impossibility theorem for risk-assessers who believe they can,
in an objective, unequivocal sense, sum the preferences of individuals and find a policy that follows the preference of the people. See
also Lave and Romer (1983). The logic of welfare based upon individual rational choice, having been shown defective, it must be a
good time to press an alternative research angle, the study of the
relation between social processes and shared values. (See Douglas,
Douglas, and Thompson 1983.)

The formal analysis of rationality presents the subjects with
clearly separated facts and values. The attitude surveys study
values but do not ask questions about how values are generated.
The attribution theorists assume that nothing need be known
about the social processes that generate and sustain patterns of
value. Concept formation is rightly taken to be the distinctively
human cognitive process that permits speech. The studies of concept formation look toward children's learning abilities and to-

ward the early stages of acquiring linguistic skills. The social processes in which children are involved are rudimentary and necessarily fragmented. Concept formation for adults involved in standardized social situations is mainly studied by anthropologists in foreign places. It will be a long time before psychological research can contribute to understanding highly socialized cognitive processes such as risk perception.

Cognitive psychology in its origins was close to animal psychology. The basic assumption in studies of animal cognition is that the organism's perceptual skills are part of its adaptation to its physical environment. Its perceptions are cued to survival in every sense—reproductive survival of the species, survival of the flock, herd, or hive if social animals are concerned, and individual requirements for feeding, mating, shelter, and security. The biological experimentation on perception assumes the animals' behavior to have adaptive value. The style of the experiments in human psychology is similar: Inputs of information are checked against outputs of performance. But though the work on human perception is modeled on animal psychology, it lacks the grand theoretical framework. There is no overall theoretical structure which qualifies the evolutionary paradigm of animal perception to suit the human condition.

The environment of an animal is much modified by its activity. This is even more true of humans. But a fundamental difference is that the humans' experience of their environment is mediated by conceptual categories which are fabricated in social intercourse. For both animals and humans, the physical objects are already coded by assumptions which come from the perceiving mechanism's side of the line. For the animals, the physical conditions are a direct object of perceptual activity, but for humans this line between perceiver and perceived is problematical. For humans the coding is not genetically controlled; cultural constraints intervene. There is the shared community work of agreeing on the categories in which the world is known. Individual perceivers incorporate into their cognitive apparatus some major classifications of the physical environment which arise from social intercourse. Take, for example, the line between nature and culture; to any individual perceiver it is given; for the analyst it must be recognized as a cultural construct.

People are said to take the threat of natural disasters more calmly, with less sense of injustice and less desire for retribution than when they are victims of man-made disaster. But no one asks how the line is drawn. (See chapter 5.) It is taken for granted that everyone can recognize that a typhoon or earthquake is a natural disaster. Recently, Amartya K. Sen (1981) has demonstrated that though meteoric conditions and harvest failures are certainly natural events, they are not necessarily large-scale disasters. Whether disaster ensues depends to a large extent on how the event is interpreted. His analysis of the conditions leading up to the major famines in Bengal, Calcutta, Sahel, and Ethiopia show that there is a false belief in responsible circles that famines have natural causes in "food availability deficits." Consequently, administrative action is directed by this myth. In case after case, inspired by the FAD theory, regulations seek to stop exports out of threatened areas but actually prevent food from getting to where it is already needed. Price restrictions encourage food hoarding; price rises do the same. All the time that eyes are fixed on food availability, they are averted from the economic and legal structures whose collapse is the main cause of famines occurring, even with good harvests and large available stocks of food. In Sen's judgment, the administrative focus on the physical fact gives rise to a mistaken theory that famine is caused by natural disasters. (See also Garcia 1982.)

It seems that social construction and consensus greatly influence human perceptions. This being so, they will be more easily destabilized than animal perceptions, and we can expect extra stabilizing processes—the sense of subjective immunity, for one—to be at work. A distinctive program for human cognitive psychology would take special interest in how the classifications of the world are formed, how they threaten to disintegrate, and how certain social processes shore them up. Questions of this kind do not get a hearing because of a strong moral and political bias among psychologists against institutional constraints on individual behavior. The opposite bias would be equally prejudicial to research. But a neutral, open attitude to social influences for stability is necessary for developing a balanced view of the individual's relation to society. Donald Campbell (1975) has recognized and rebuked a professional bias against social factors influencing perception. Questions about the survival of human social forms would parallel those questions that relate animal cognition to species survival. Questions about concept formation and learning would be set in a context of sociological comparison. There would need to be typologies of stable social processes and the kind of moral commitments which sustain them. Such a theoretical shift would modify the entrenched ideas that facts can be clearly separated from values. There cannot be a serious study of perception that does not recognize social concerns that influence selective attention.

Selective Attention

In the 1940s cognitive psychology was in dialogue with sociology, particularly through Egon Frankel-Brunswick's interest in intolerance (especially ethnic intolerance) as a personality trait (1948, 1949, 1954). But the work that this stimulated on the authoritarian personality was less experimental and more inclined toward social theory (Adorno, 1950). Though the work had initially been influenced by neuropsychology, the two streams of social and psychological theory drew apart. The central work of Donald Hebb in perception theory emphasized attention as a selectivity of response. He argued that traditionally psychologists searched for a property of the stimulus which by itself determines the ensuing response; against the old tradition "almost without exception, psychologists have recognized the existence of the selective central factor that reinforces now one response, now another." He complained that in spite of this professional agreement, there is a problem of carrying it to its logical conclusion: "an incomplete line of thought starts out preoccupied with stimulus or stimulus configuration as the source and control of action, eventually runs into the facts of attention and so on, and then simply agrees that attention is an important fact, without recognizing that this is inconsistent with one's earlier assumptions" (Hebb 1949:4–5). In risk perception researchers agree that attention selectivity is the real issue, and at the same time go on categorizing the configurations of stimuli. Suggestions for how relevant differences in social experience could be identified for further such cognitive experimentation are given in Douglas (1978). This approach was formulated in Douglas (1966) as an explicit development of the 1940s and 1950s work in perception psychology referred to above.

Social structure is a moral system; social accountability creates the main lines of cost-benefit payoffs and produces the different ways of categorizing the physical world. As with animals, human attention is focused by the concern to survive. But for humans, survival involves the human kind of communicating, and this involves establishing the conceptual categories for public discourse. A cognitive psychology that ignored the process would seem to trivialize its own project. It would certainly disqualify itself for considering risk acceptability.

Summary: Nineteenth-century theorizing about risk separated gambling from other risk-taking. Within the modern theory of choice, risk aversion and risk-seeking are now presented within an integrated theory. This chapter points out some limitations of the theory of choice for the question of ascertaining public levels of tolerance for risk.

The theory of choice applies logic to the act of choosing. The rational argument is one that is not self-contradictory and likewise the rational choice. To be rational, one choice does not negate another. Rational behavior implies some ordering of alternatives in terms of relative desirability. The logic of choice concerns non-contradictory or ordered preferences. In science, probabilities are assessments of the reliability of expectations about events. Probabilities also figure prominently in the theory of choice. It makes a lot of difference to a decision if the alternatives involve choosing between a certainty and an uncertainty, or between a low and a high probability. The variance of the probability constitutes the risk element. In the seventeenth and eighteenth centuries theorizing about risk concerned the mathematics of gambling, and so the focus was precisely on the structure of probabilities as a whole. In the nineteenth century the theorizing about risk shifted from gaming to the risks of economic enterprise and particularly to the probabilities of loss. Inevitably, the theory of risk has come to be emphasized as the probability of not reaching an objective—with a negative judgment passed against the very long shot gamble for high stakes. The traditional arguments have been

41

about the relation between the objectively calculated (or mathematical) probabilities and values as compared with the subjective estimations of the rational agent; about the most useful definition of rationality that can be devised for understanding the logic of choice; and about the adequacy of the match between this definition and actual behavior.

Most of the path-finding work on risk, determining the way it is now discussed, has been put in hand before the recent grave concern about risks from technology. It started with the publication in 1944 of *The Theory of Games* by Von Neumann and Morgenstern and emerged complete as to its main axioms and theorems in a brief five years between 1948 and 1953. Later developments have been more in the nature of fine-tuning, criticisms, and improvements of different parts of a formidably rigorous conceptual apparatus. Subsequently, decision theory has been applied to practical questions of military strategy. There has also been some effort to apply these methods to the risks of industrial technology. Utility theory has been applied, with perplexing results, to assessing the compensation for a life or the claims of unborn generations. There is a real question as to how well the whole theoretical system may be adapted to producing answers to public policy questions about risks arising from nuclear power or toxic industrial wastes. Yet these are the kinds of questions the new subdiscipline has been formed to answer.

Every choice we make is beset with uncertainty. That is the basic condition of human knowledge. A great deal of risk analysis is concerned with trying to turn uncertainties into probabilities. What seems to be in each case a purely technical exercise quickly becomes one that rests directly upon the philosophical foundations of inference. Isaac Levi's "Brief Sermon on Assessing Accident Risks in U.S. Commercial Nuclear Power Plants," is a close examination of the statistical procedures used by the Nuclear Regulatory Commission's *Reactor Safety Study* (1975). The appendices to that report discuss the difficulties involved in making evaluations of the probabilities and the methods employed in meeting them. Little could the engineers who wrote the report have expected to find an epistemologist question their choices and particularly their reasons for them.

The authors of the report, however, did seem anxious to ground judgments of credal probability on judgments as

42

to which of rival statistical hypotheses concerning the objective chance distribution of failure rates is correct. In the face of insufficient data, the authors did not conclude that they should suspend judgment between the rival statistical hypotheses and look to their credal state for the various seriously possible rivals for help in determining via direct inference which credal state to adopt. That approach would have led to an indeterminate state of credal judgment concerning failure rates. [p. 441]

Levi then goes on to relate their methodological choice to the assumptions of Quine and other epistemologists, and concludes with the moral that we should learn to suspend judgment and not pretend to precision we lack (Levi 1980).

A risky situation is one governed by known probabilities. If not enough is known about the probabilities, we are dealing with uncertainties. Risk-taking in its most obvious form is the gamble. A risk-taker prefers the small probability of a large gain and the large probability of a small loss over a certain income. The risk-averse buys insurance: that is preferring a certain small loss (the premium) to avert the small chance of a large loss. Insurance reduces the variants of future probabilities.

Nineteenth-century economics, while it recognized that some risk-taking is compatible with rational economic behavior, condemned the gamble. Strong disapproval emanates from Marshall's language about the gambler (1890). Following Bentham, he declares the pleasures of gambling to be "impure," since "experience shows how they are likely to engender a restless, feverish character, unsuited for steady work as well as for the higher and more solid pleasures of life."

This moral attitude and the theory of diminishing marginal utility reinforce one another. If an additional dollar has less value than the last one gained, then a 50/50 chance of winning or losing a dollar will be unattractive to the rational agent: He will feel the loss of a dollar that he already has with a pain that will exceed the pleasure to be gained from winning an additional one. (Indeed, most people are not attracted by this wager.) For the school of marginal analysis, fair gambling will always entail economic loss: Only a fool would engage in it. So gambling lies outside their definition of rational economic behavior. However, it has to be recognized that business activity entails risks. Then the question for economic policy becomes how to persuade risk-

43

averse citizens to assume necessary risks. The answer is that special rewards have to be offered to the risk-bearer, an intellectual justification for high profits for the entrepreneur. To be fair to Marshall, his arguments still make good sense in the revised theory of utility: A low probability of winning is not an attractive game unless the stakes are very high.

According to Friedman and Savage (1948), the moral judgment against gamblers was not the main inspiration for the bias in the theory but rather the intuitive appeal of the theory of diminishing marginal utility. The idea of diminishing marginal utility originally had a simple physicalist base. It is obvious that the satisfaction to be gained from eating one loaf of bread declines after the second, and even more after the fifth and sixth. This is just as true of any eating or drinking or taking of medicine. The body's declining satisfaction may be the analogy for the declining value of clothing or recreational housing, but it is only a metaphor. For most goods, what diminishes with increasing expenditures on them is the socially approved outlets for enjoying them, and this is especially clear for the declining psychological value of money.

Early utility theory rested on the idea of an absolute cardinal value for the idea of utility—such that it could be measured, summed, and compared, an idea beset with difficulty. Economic theory soon shifted away from cardinal utility, through the work of Edgeworth, Fisher, and Pareto on indifference curve analysis. Pareto (1848–1923) was particularly influential in purging all trace of utilitarianism from the foundations of economic theory. Indirectly, this meant that risk-taking came in for less attention than it had in the period when it was an integral part of utility analysis. The 1940s see the big shift in the theory of choice, which puts risk right back into the new revised version of utility analysis that is still current. In *The Theory of Games* Von Neumann and Morgenstern show that the theoretical developments away from cardinal values and in favor of ordinal rankings of satisfactions can be compatible with giving a numerical value to the relative satisfaction or utility to be expected from different choices. Risk is now reincorporated in the analysis of decisions, since expected utility is made to depend on the attractiveness of a particular combination of probabilities and values. Incidentally, the theory of choice gets a big push in the old direction. Going much further back than to Marshallian utility, the new approach

44

hails as its starting point the formula proposed by Daniel Bernoulli in 1738 to solve a gambling problem.

The St. Petersburg Game

The game is simple. A fair coin is tossed until a head appears; then the game stops. The player is paid two ducats for every toss. The puzzle is to know how much he should be prepared to pay for the gamble. Intuitively, he never wants to pay much for it. But the mathematical expectation of the game is infinite, so on a "rational" calculation he ought to be ready to pay any finite amount for the chance of a game. What has gone wrong? Through the centuries, a continuous flow of solutions has been proposed for the St. Petersburg game. Bernoulli's answer depends on the difference between the high mathematical expectation and the low psychological value set by the player on the sum that could be won. However, this narrowing of the discrepancy still leaves a large gap between the ordinary person's intuition and what Bernoulli thinks is a reasonable price. Another set of solutions has pointed out that the person offering to sell the gamble is a sham if he pretends he really could pay out an infinite sum. But this again falls short of the ordinary person's intuition, which is not that he will ruin the bank, but that he will himself gain very little indeed. More convincing are the solutions based on the habit of discarding low probabilities (Gorovitz 1979). In summarizing the immense literature on the paradox, G. J. Stigler mentions some far-out solutions which evoke some of the contemporary literature on background natural risks cited in chapter 2. "Perhaps the most amusing solution was one by Buffon—that all probabilities smaller than .001 are equal to zero (because this was the probability of dying during the day for a man of fifty six, which was commonly treated as negligible)." Stigler explodes the paradox by remarking that to the economist the most surprising aspect of this debate "is the mathematician's chief requisite of a solution: that a finite value be found for the value of the game" (Stigler 1969).

Bernoulli's solution was to develop an index for the declining marginal utility of money. No wonder that he is regarded as the founding ancestor of the modern utility theory. By 1950 all seems set for the steady expansion and consolidation which actually does take place.

Five Exploratory Years of Risk in the New Utility Framework

1948: M. Friedman and L. J. Savage, "The Utility Analysis of Choices Involving Risk." This is an opening salvo in a debate inspired by Von Neumann and Morgenstern. The theory of choice

45

can now integrate choice among certain outcomes with choice among risks. It starts from the hypothesis that a consuming unit decides in favor of a gamble or in favor of a certainty according to the difference between the expected utility of the gamble compared with the expected utility of the certainty. It assumes that the utility function rises with income. It offers further subsidiary hypotheses about risk-aversiveness based on relative size of income.

1951: Kenneth Arrow, "Alternative Approaches to the Theory of Choice in Risk-Taking Situations." The theory of choice has been recently affected by three new developments: (a) in utility theory (see 1948 above), (b) in the theory of statistical inference, and (c) in Shackle's rejection of probability calculation and his theory of uncertain anticipation. Arrow's article deals most extensively with problems in the foundations of probability insofar as they affect the theory of choice.

1952: Centre National de Recherche, Colloquy on Risk, Paris. Papers presented anticipate major work by Samuelson ("Utility, Preference and Probability"), Savage ("An Axiomatization of Reasonable Behavior in Face of Uncertainty"), Friedman ("The Expected Utility Hypothesis and the Measurement of Utility"); M. Allais presents a controversial series of papers, one of which is published in the next year.

1953: Maurice Allais, "Le Comportement de l'homme rationel devant le risque: Critique des postulats et axiomes de l'école Americaine."

The passionate attack which Maurice Allais launches in 1952 and 1953 against "the American School" seems to come as a surprise. The editor of *Econometrica* takes the unusual precaution of noting that customary procedures of editorial consulting have failed to clear up misunderstandings on the main points at issue: "The paper is published as it now stands on the author's responsibility." In "the American School" Allais includes as leaders L. J. Savage and Paul Samuelson and names other statisticians and decision theorists, some of whom he claims started out on the side of error but recanted before his article went to press. His main objection is to their reliance on Bernoulli's theorem. The source of his griefs against the new Bernoullians is his desire to see the development of a pure theory of risk. The essence of risk-taking lies in the structure of the probabilities, their variance. A prudent individual seeks less, the risk-taker prefers more variance. A theory of decision-making that takes the mean of the distribution of probabilities disregards the very thing that risk-taking is all about, the distribution itself. Apart from developing a theory of risk that loses sight of the real risk experience, Allais suspects

46

that the Bernoullians are even telling us when it is rational to be prudent and when to take risks. Of course this is what decision theory is devised for, but he considers it a preposterous teaching, especially when some of the postulates inserted into the definition of rationality are highly restrictive and counterintuitive. Above all, Bernoulli's log-linear index of declining utility does not correspond to the sudden discontinuities of focus which characterize quite rational decision-making. It is perfectly rational to want a particular sum no less and no more. It is not always rational to maximize: Suppose that a traveler is stranded in Marseilles and urgently needs to return to Paris; if he has only 100 francs in his pocket, the game that gives him the best probability of winning the price of his return ticket will be more advantageous to him than following the rule of maximizing his mathematical expectations of gains.

Allais invents a game which he proposes to the Americans. It is a trap which, if they fall into it, will conclusively disprove one of Savage's axioms. They all fall into the trap, and Allais wins the round.

Allais's Paradox

Allais's game is a paradox if you accept Savage's independence axiom and if you also violate the axiom in playing the game. Yakov Amihud (1979) points out that this particular axiom is not necessary for the derivation of the expected utility theorem; furthermore, Allais has misinterpreted the use of the definition of rationality in the Von Neumann–Morgenstern utility theory; their idea of rationality is not intended to be descriptive of rational behavior but normative, given acceptance of the underlying axioms. The independence principle concerns the coherence of an ordering of preferences. It asserts that if two alternatives have a common outcome, then the ordering of the alternatives should be independent of the value of that common outcome. The emphasis is upon the commitment to the particular outcome. Whereas Allais insists that a given outcome does not retain its relative attractiveness when the rest of the problem has changed, for instance, a change in the probabilities will change the ordering of preferences. This game has been played many times over with ingenious variations. This summary is from Slovic and Tversky (1974), in which references will be found to the other versions.

Imagine the following two decision situations—each involving a pair of gambles:

Situation X	Probability of Winning	Amount to Win
Gamble 1	100%	$1,000,000
Gamble 2	10	5,000,000
	89	1,000,000
	1	0
Situation Y		
Gamble 3	11	1,000,000
	89	0
Gamble 4	10	5,000,000
	90	0

Savage's independence principle implies that if one chooses Gamble 1 in situation X, one also goes on to choose Gamble 3 that gives the same outcome in situation Y. And if one's order of preference is for Gamble 2 in situation X (10 percent chance of winning $5,000,000) one would go on to choose Gamble 4 for situation Y. But in practice, the subjects of this experiment tend to go for the certainty of $1,000,000 in situation X, then to take a breath and decide in situation Y that between two highly probable outcomes of winning nothing and two minuscule chances of either $1,000,000 or $5,000,000, it would be better to go for the high stakes. The pressure of certainty has shifted the order of preferences.

This game has become almost as famous as the St. Petersburg paradox. A large volume of essays (Allais and Hagen 1979) comments upon its implications. The most direct benefit from it to the theory of risk has been the work of Daniel Kahneman and Amos Tversky in a detailed overhaul of expected utility theory as a descriptive model of decision-making under risk (1979). This work approaches decisions at two levels: the kinds of choices between gambles that people are apt to make and the editing process that tends to be applied to the form in which choices are expressed. The theory, called prospect theory, is the result of axiomatization and psychological experimentation. The "certainty effect" shown in Allais's original experiment refines the weighting of certainties, probabilities, and values. The "isolation effect" is the coding of a complex problem which shows that when there is a dependency among events, the choice between prospects is not solely determined by the probabilities of final states but by reference to a starting point. Individuals are more influenced by changes from some given base line than by total sums to be won or lost. Consequently, attention has to be paid to the shifts of reference. This is very relevant to the safety-first issues discussed later. It has always been recognized that risk-seeking increases with probabilities of loss and risk aversion for probabilities of gain; one prefers the largest variance of probabilities for the former, the smallest for the latter. But this "mirror-effect" was not systematized within utility theory until Kahneman and Tversky worked out appropriate weightings for prospects of loss and gain. So, they have integrated gambling with other forms of risk-seeking overlooked in utility theory.

Prospect theory supports Allais's general case by demonstrating
that attitudes toward risk are determined jointly by values and
probabilities and not solely by the utility function. In particular,
Kahneman and Tversky maintain that decision theory, by asssum-
ing that persons formulate their decision problems in terms of final
assets (instead of relative gains and losses), does essentially eliminate risk-seeking in the domain of losses.

So Allais was right. And now his main objective is won. He
can point to a new theory of risk which focuses on risk-taking as
such and does not sweep important risky choices under the car-
pet, saying that they fall outside the domain of rational behavior.
The matter could rest here. Prospect theory does fulfill the
difficult demand for a sufficiently abstract level of argument that
can still relate to the practical situations of choice. It accounts for
the stranded traveler's concern just to win his return fare to
Paris: He is not looking at the final outcome of the game, but at
some nearer reference point.

Nonetheless, for good reasons the pure theory of rational choice
has little guidance for the contemporary questions about industrial risk. The first reason is that these concerns have to do with
the ends or objectives of rational behavior, and the theory, strictly
speaking, has nothing to say about ends. One could suppose it is
absurd to turn to this body of theory for guidance about the
public acceptability of technological risks. It can say a lot about
the coherence between different subsidiary levels of choice once
the major goal has been given. But we should recognize that
there is a limit to the possibility of goals being made coherent
with one another. Living in society forces rational beings to tolerate a lot of incoherence. Living in an arbitrary political system is
a further impediment to pursuing a coherent set of ends. These
problems deeply engage Western philosophers. It still remains
plausible that a fully coherent moral system, though a logical
ideal, is a practical impossibility. (The sages of the East evade the
paradox by teaching nonattachment.) Lastly, there are important
risks which are taken and which never enter into the process of
decision-making, because they have not been perceived or because (as in the case of the erosion of soils in the Midwest of
America) they are perceived, but not counted as decisionable.

Utility theory has more to say about risk. Allais's insistence
that big discontinuities in preference be accounted for implies
something about the utility function onto which risk preferences

49

ultimately have to be mapped. Risks cannot be treated as equivalent to each other. This is the mistake that Chauncey Starr made in trying to lump all risks under a single measure, such as more or fewer days in the expectation of life affected by risks from carcinogenic soft drinks, road accidents, and sports. Perhaps it would open some important issues to try to construct a risk tree, something like a cultural utility tree (Strotz 1957) whose branches consist of groups of comparable gambles. Each culture would have a risk tree of a particular shape, corresponding to its established levels of acceptability. But what would the tree be constructed from? Not from a hierarchy of physical needs, such as an Engel curve for the steady demand for bread or food in workmen's budgets. The physical basis of wants has already been too much of a distraction to economic theory (Douglas and Isherwood 1978). Chauncey Starr was on the right track when he distinguished voluntarily assumed risks from those imposed by others. A pattern of social demands needs to be identified with the pattern underlying risk acceptability if risk intolerance is to be understood.

Consider again the stranded traveler. Why on earth does he need to rush away? It may be that in Paris his father is dying. Or it may be his wedding day, or he has to sit an exam; or his landlord will foreclose his mortgage unless he comes. Whatever good reasons we can propose, they all amount to other people demanding his presence. If it were not for social pressures, he might just as well stay in Marseilles, take a job, and play out the full maximizing strategy that decision theory prescribes. One of the first branches of the risk tree could well correspond to the amount of calendrical discriminations requiring a person to be in set places at set times on pain of forfeit, because this source of complexity in social organization makes a lot of difference to preferred risk strategies.

Complexity

Under the aegis of the Russell Sage Foundation, a few anthropologists combined with a computer scientist to work out a measure of relative complexity of social organization that could provide a basis for comparisons of this kind. See Douglas (1984) and also Douglas and Gross (1981).

50

Friedman and Savage (1948) have offered some interesting suggestions about the way that the social organization impinges on private attitudes to risk. They suppose two qualitatively different socioeconomic levels, one high- and one low-income, and a transitional area in between. Then increases in income that raise the relative position of a consumer unit in its own class, but do not shift it out, yield diminishing marginal utility. In this imaginary economy, the shape of the utility curve is convex for the lower-income and higher-income groups, but not for the middle segment. Because of declining marginal utility a low-income unit will be averse to small gambles, perhaps averse to all gambles, though possibly attracted to a fair gamble that offers a small chance of a large gain. Units in the transitional segment are tempted by every small gamble and by some large ones: "They will be continually subjecting themselves to risk" and so they are likely to move either up into the higher segment or down into the lower one according to the luck of the gamble. This gives a basis for the authors to speculate upon the stability of relative income status in both upper- and lower-income groups and to postulate considerable instability in the status of units in the middle-income class. They go on to imagine an economy in which the utility curve does not yield diminishing marginal utility.

In such a case the upper-income consumer units "would take almost any gamble and those on high incomes today would almost certainly not have high incomes tomorrow" (Friedman and Savage 1948:303). An we can add that if everyone in the upper-income group was taking big gambles all the time, standardized public attitudes would be in alignment: There would be a culture whose tolerance for risk-taking would be very high. So utility analysis can be a source of ideas about the relation of values to economic structure and about risks from technology, though as an intellectual resource it is not much exploited for this purpose. These speculations are similar to those based on empirical research on social conditions favoring risk-taking.

Risk-Taking by Social Class

There is no consensus among scholars regarding the relationship between social rank and risk-taking. While Rogers (1982) and Rogers and Shoemaker (1971) assert a positive correlation between the two variables, Cancian (1967, 1972) argues for a negative correlation across all social ranks. To the extent that in real life upper classes enjoy a certain degree of security, the negative relationship between risk-taking and rank is likely to be observed only in the middle class. Though Cancian claims that the data on Mayan corn farmers support his contentions, Gartrell (1972, 1973) questions the validity of his findings both on methodological and substantive grounds.

The debate might have been less inconclusive if the questions had been explicitly researched within Friedman and Savage's theoretical framework. We can ask what social or economic conditions affect the shape of the utility curve. New technology or expanding resources (or both combined) can burst through the cultural controls on what may acceptably be spent on food, clothing, housing, and holidays. The argument depends on identifying a social-economic environment in which publicly standardized constraints on new forms of enjoyment are weak. But what reduces the constraints? A first answer is that any major disturbance of social boundaries and hierarchies will have this effect.

Friedman and Savage (1948) write as if one obviously would prefer to escape the stuffiness of the closed community. They may be right, but they may be wrong. They claim that

> an unskilled worker may prefer the certainty of an income about the same as that of the majority of unskilled workers to an actuarily fair gamble that would at best make him one of the most prosperous, unskilled workers and at worst one of the least prosperous. Yet he may jump at a chance of a fair gamble that offers a small chance of lifting him out of the class of unskilled workers and into the "middle" or "upper" class, even though it is more likely than the other gamble to make him one of the least prosperous unskilled workers. [p. 299]

This is disputable. A big sociological literature discusses the reluctance of the lower-income groups to buy education as a long-shot gamble for entry into the upper-income brackets. It may be very worrying to contemplate a leap out of a defined social context where there are limits to the honors that can be won into a normless world where anything is permissible. Durkheim (1952:246–76) thought that this very shift was liable to bring on a suicidal depression. Admittedly untidier than the strictly axiomatized theory of choice and admittedly highly speculative, these subsidiary hypotheses about the effects of the economy on risk aversion lead straight into mainstream sociology. At very least, there should be a debate backed by research on the kinds of correlation here proposed.

52

Chapter 5   Natural Risks

Summary: This chapter argues that the cultural processes which select certain kinds of dangers for attention work through institutional procedures for allocating responsibility. Blaming the victim, blaming the victim's parents, or blaming the outsider are well-known strategies.

There is a current misleading assumption about how dangers from nature are perceived. Physical signs of the typhoon or earthquake appear first as small spots on the horizon; interpreting them is full of uncertainty; as they approach, misperceptions pile up and the final disaster comes as a surprise—stochastically foreseen by the expert but not by the victims. Such a physical idea of perception and the passive idea of the public is a carryover from the earlier work in the sociology of disaster where the focus was not on perception at all.

Disaster Research

In the twenty years from 1942 to 1962 (starting with the NASNR Committee), disaster studies focused upon assessing impact, rescue, and recovery (see Torry 1979a). An exception is Stephen Withey's study (1962) of how fragmentary and ambiguous signs of danger produce different responses. His definition of effective warning as a function of the amount of information to be contradicted is close to a statement about culturally standardized expectations of disaster.

53

A truly human ecological approach to disaster which incorporates organizational models of the local social-natural system would also take into account anticipatory and remedial institutions which give resilience to a human population.

This is more in accord with what is understood elsewhere about perception. It is also compatible with the lessons of anthropology about how dangers are allocated between natural and man-made causes. Here it is argued that disasters are not quite unforeseen. Even brand-new forms of menace, without having been anticipated, can be labeled and slotted into existing categories of responsibility. Uncertainty about human reactions will have been sedulously reduced by well-known procedures, proverbs, and moral maxims. Some prior perception of the probability of danger will have been incorporated into the institutional structures. The people are already alerted to the first symptoms of danger, but their attention is focused on moral or political weaknesses that they expect will escalate the damage. Dangers are culturally selected for recognition—not all dangers, but some. The response is precoded in terms of appropriate action such as public inquiry, punishment, or withdrawal of support. Risk perception questionnaires cannot tap this level of awareness: First, they suppose the line between nature and culture is something given in nature; second, they treat facts as separate from values; and third, they take the institutional structure for granted. Above all, it is beyond the scope of a questionnaire to tap into underlying assumptions, even supposing the survey designer is interested in looking for them.

In excuse, some would claim that the anthropologist's insights into stable cultures are irrelevant to modern society. After all, we are facing totally unprecedented technological dangers. The reply to this excuse is yes; if the focus is on the physical danger, the insights of anthropology would be irrelevant. However, the focus ought not to be on the danger but on the institutions if we are interested in public perception. The functional approach of anthropology insists that the expectation of dangers tends to be institutionalized so that it stabilizes and generally supports the local regime, whatever it may be. The analysis is exactly based on Durkheim's analysis of the social functions of crime and closely follows his idea of the sacred (1933, esp. chap. 2; see also Douglas 1966). For Durkheim it does not so much matter what the crimes are, so long as they are heinous enough to arouse passions on the side of law and order. Even brand-new crimes will be institutionalized to the same public service. Genocide may strike us as a new kind of crime, but it still goes into an expanded category of murder. Likewise, one could expect that even brand-new varieties of danger will get the same institutionalizing treatment. Then it becomes urgent to ask what kind of institutional structures support what kind of perceptions of danger. Community-wide institutions are more sensitive to community-wide threats, such as drought or epidemic. Domestic institutions are more sensitive to local disasters, such as loss of livestock or a shooting accident.

In developing this approach, some explicit assumptions are needed. First, we can assume that institution-building and institution-maintaining is a rational process in which individuals negotiate their goals and complex choices so as to reach some degree of institutional viability; we can assume also that moral principles as well as logical coherence are invoked in the monitoring aspects of this process. Furthermore, we can assume that insofar as they agree at all on goals, the constituent members of an institution are also incorporating agreement on things to be avoided. Agreement on the specific kinds of losses to which they are averse is one of the topics of members' negotiations with one another. They may want protection against cattle thieves or irrigation to alleviate possibility of drought or dikes to be maintained against flooding. Consequently, some recognized risks are written into the constitution along with common goals. We can safely assume that institutions stop curiosity as well as reward learning. Since a focus on one kind of danger directs attention away from others, it follows that the perceptual monitoring will not be random, but will be a function of the kind of organization that is being achieved.

Social Control of Curiosity

The concept of culture as shared assumptions and values implies something like a patterning of ideas: When some problems and solutions are foregrounded to be available, by the same token others are pushed into the background. Basil Bernstein (1971, 1973, 1975) has analyzed this process of coding experience in modern industrial society. There is a close relation between the internal organization of schooling institutions and the kinds of curriculum they promote, and the scholarly values and attitudes that are their product. This analysis is a refinement in Durkheimian tradition of Weber's idea of rationality in institutions. Study of risk perception would benefit from being related to a strong critical tradition in the history and sociology of science led by Robert K. Merton (1968b). When a risk is taken with bending the social rules, and the gamble fails, the misfortune that falls on the risk-taker is an example of the famous self-fulfilling prophecy that Merton analyzed in 1948. Likewise, his analyses of scientists' rejection of important information. To place risk perception within such a perspective is not something outlandish or novel but a matter of introducing different parts of the same subject to each other (Barber 1961).

The next step is to assume that most institutions tend to solve some of their organizational problems through public allocation of blame. Naturally, these problems and the blaming procedures vary according to the kind of organizations. Lastly, some machinery for renewing members' commitment to the institution's objectives is activated by the threat of disaster.

Under these procedures, nature can be made into a sensitive gauge of morality—sometimes seen as a heavy-handed judge of moral disorder in general, as when earthquakes and typhoons are held to punish the whole people for their sins, and sometimes as a discriminating assessor of hidden private crimes. Since this is known to be a tendency of primitive religion, some examples will help to lower that distracting old division between us, the moderns, and them, the ancients or the primitives. We also use nature's powers as a technique of social coercion.

First consider the possibility of blaming the victim for his own misfortune, the prime type of a self-fulfilling prophecy. When the victim has died this strategy stops scapegoating of living persons. It quickly ends feuding and allows commissions of inquiry to conclude with a verdict of death by natural causes or misadventure or human error, thus invoking nature to let everyone off the hook. It is a familiar Marxist criticism of how class hegemony brings the machinery of justice into its service. For blaming the victim is effective for silencing indictments of the whole social system. The unmarried mother used to be blamed as if she were the sole procreator of her child (Donzelot 1979). The sick person gets blame for ill-health (NaVarro 1975, 1977). Nature does not lend herself simply to the prosecution of the class war. Blaming the victim is a hand-washing ploy good for all sorts of occasions. When the dead pilot can be blamed for the error that crashed his plane, there is no need to inquire further into the adequacy of the traffic controls or the plane's fitness for flying: Everyone is content to leave it at that, except the Pilots' Association, which finds it very damaging to their profession. Throughout Africa a traditional belief associated leprosy with incest. This painful, unsightly, and lingering disease puts a burden of compassion on the friends of the leper. An element of hand-washing lurks in the whispered allegation of scandalous sex as its origin. When a mother dies in childbirth, in many countries her adultery is considered a possible cause of her death: The efforts to help her in labor focus on exhorting her to confess so as to be saved by the appropriate medicines. Deaths in childbirth are warnings posted by nature to women tempted to infidelity. The nineteenth-century idea of the fragile feminine nature and of female vulnerability to insanity helped to secure women's compliance with their passive role in marriage arrangements (Skultans 1975). Thus, well-labeled, natural vulnerabilities point to certain classes of people as likely victims; their state of being "at risk" justifies bringing them under control. In modern industrial society the poor are nutritionally at risk, and pregnant, poor women especially so. Their vulnerability entitles society at large to deflect blame by imposing close restrictions on their shopping and diet as conditions of their receiving a modicum of aid. If they or their babies are eventually struck down, their rejection of official help explains why they themselves are to blame (Deutsch 1982).

Nature is even more effective in ensuring moral conformity when the blame is taken away from the victims and placed on the shoulders of the nearest and dearest. Close kin are stopped from complaining because they know that they themselves are the objects of reproach. So parents of a handicapped child wonder what they did to cause their child's sorrow—something callous at birth? or later? In certain African societies this tendency is made more pointed by connecting particular disasters with specific misbehavior: A warrior has a poor chance in battle if his wife is unfaithful while he is at risk; when he comes home wounded, his family knows whom to suspect. Childbirth and battle are real dangers. But dangers can be fabricated to lay responsibilities precisely in the right quarter. In Britain in the 1950s, when middle-class wives started to defy custom, get highly educated, and go out to work, Bowlby's theory of maternal deprivation (1951) had an enormous success: Clinics explained to anxious young mothers the meaning of early imprinting on greylag

57

geese and warned how nature would lash back at them causing their child loss of identity and incapacity to love if they persisted in what working-class mothers had long been used to doing—going out to work (Ainsworth 1962). A loveless child—such a sanction is analogous to telling African mothers that they will lose their small babies. Nature's threat to their dear ones shows them where their duty lies.

These cases of nature being used to keep women in control give a false impression of sexist bias. The father can also define his rights to his wife and children by emphasizing his own importance at childbirth. Where no dowries or marriage settlements make his status clear (as in many hunting and gathering societies) the custom of couvade stresses his physical connection with birth and safe delivery. In the last hundred years we have seen a revolution in our recent Western attitudes to the father's presence at his own child's delivery. The child will have a healthier birth and happier personality if the father plays a part in the great event that used to be the sole responsibility of womenfolk. It would be hard to maintain that this change has nothing to do with defining the obligations of paternity when the couple is faced with a weakened marriage tie, increased cost of children's education, and problems of affiliation and alimony (Douglas 1975; Paige and Paige 1981; Lewis 1982).

Whether nature is named as judge or victim, the process is highly political. The idea of nature is being used to bring pressure. Industrial pollution is the case in which mother nature threatens to succumb. This is the most powerful coercion of all. "If you children don't stop, I will have one of my heart attacks." Mutual accountability also involves nature's intervention at a higher political level. Frequently, an African leader claims access to the ancestors who will be expected to punish political disobedience by withholding rain or sending blight. But the followers are not gullible or passive: If they do not approve of their leader, they can claim that his bad leadership, not their disaffection, has caused the disastrous weather, so they use the meteoric conditions to justify a dynastic revolution. Again, most political leaders would love to blame external enemies for all the troubles suffered by their people. But this is more difficult to maintain than blaming the victim and the victim's kin. It is a kind of abdication from responsibility which in the long run will fail to bring in the votes. The would-be leader can't go around forever wringing his hands and saying, "An enemy hath done this thing." Sometime he needs to indicate which enemy and what he proposes to do.

Keep in mind these possibilities of involving nature in the social process. It follows that levels of acceptability are set in the course of developing a social audit for the whole community. The question is not which dangers are most alarming but which explanations of misfortune are likely to function most effectively in the different kinds of society we might be able to identify. Are there some patterns to be discerned?

We have recognized for a long time that the worst dangers that can happen are already converted into well-advertised risks. The individual who takes the risk makes a trade-off between the satisfaction of revolting against social constraints and the loss caused by falling victim to some fearful natural disaster. The use of risk as a technique of coercion is not incorporated into any part of the professional discourse on risk perception. To do so would require a hypothesis of the system-maintaining functions of recognized risks. In such a discussion the system would be the social unit which uses the dangers from nature to secure compliance from its own members.

Clearly, blaming the victim is a strategy that works in one kind of context, and blaming the outside enemy, a strategy that works in another. Victim blaming facilitates internal social control; outsider blaming enhances loyalty. Both ploys would serve an intention to prevent the community from being riven by dissention. Members committed to a society founded on principles of open adversarial confrontation would not be likely to give credence to either of these stock responses to disaster. The accumulation of instances cited only shows that the incidence of misfortune is likely to be put to political uses. It remains to distinguish further the kinds of polity and the patterns of blaming and not blaming that sustain them.

Risks clamor for attention; probable dangers crowd from all sides, in every mouthful and at every step. The rational agent who attended to all of them would be paralyzed. The accepted theory of risk perception maintains that the rational principle of selection would combine the probability of an event with its value. However, people tend to fasten attention on the middle range of probabilities. High-probability dangers get overlooked. Heavy losses are entailed by risks of accidents in the home or on

the road, but it is extremely difficult to get the average house-
holder or driver to take effective precautions, such as laying down
nonslip surfaces on domestic floors or wearing seat belts in cars.
At the same time, many risks that combine heavy consequences
with low probability, such as floods and earthquakes, are ignored.
Something else is happening to fasten attention on particular
risks and to screen out perception of others. Here it is argued
that public moral judgments powerfully advertise certain risks.
The well-advertised risk generally turns out to be connected with
legitimating moral principles.

Plausibility Structures

The subject of risk acceptability can be fruitfully discussed
within the concept of legitimacy and by analyzing the processes
which legitimate ideas about the world so that they become attested facts. Berger and Luckmann (1966; Berger 1969, 1978) in
their seminal works on the social grounding of plausibility have
contrasted it with its opposite, implausibility, and have contrasted
stereotypes of primitive and modern society. At this point the discussion would be enriched by introducing varieties of legitimation
processes, and resultant varieties of world views.

The moral concern guides not just the response to risk but the
basic faculty of perception. Compare, for example, the way that
professions respond to the threat of scandal. The stronger the
professional organization, the more it will insist on doing its own
policing and punishing of its members, and the more strictly it
will draw professional lines of accreditation and the more terrible
the threat of disbarring a member at fault. The profession most
deeply concerned with its collective reputation in the world of
professions will be more inclined to protect its members and only
to publicly criticize exemplary cases of misconduct when it can
expel the defaulter.

Professional Loyalty

When an outbreak of smallpox in Birmingham in 1978 was investigated, the *Times* (January 7, 1979) observed: "The over-
whelming impression that emerges from the Shooter report is of a
group of specialists, closely linked socially and professionally, unable to criticize a colleague . . . a system designed to prevent just
such an outbreak was undermined by an accumulation of over-
sights, deceptions and cosy informalities."

By contrast, individual American doctors have in the last decade become more and more exposed to litigation. Forced to be fully accountable in matters of great uncertainty and life and death consequence, not surprisingly American "physicians seem to favor worst-case scenarios." Williamson (1981) holds that such a siege mentality contributed to the swine flu fiasco. The institutional supports for two different attitudes to risk-taking in public medicine could be systematically investigated.

In the United States the Disease Control Center has to work with a looser association of professional medicine and a weaker bureaucratic community than exist in Britain. In Britain there is likely to be more mutual shielding of doctors from criticism. More professional cover-up means more professional boldness. One would expect more danger from untested drugs going on the market in Britain and more speed in getting the green light to develop and market a new beneficial discovery. When it came to taking nationwide precautions against a suspected new attack of the devastating swine flu in 1976, the Americans and British specialists read the same evidence for totally different conclusions. The British took the risk that swine flu was not a threat and the Americans instituted nationwide vaccination, but the swine flu threat did not develop. This suggests that protecting from criticism and victim-blaming, when they go with a strong communal organization, lead to less risk aversion. A community can take a bold public policy decision in favor of risk-seeking if it is strong enough to protect the decision-makers from blame. On the other hand, a hierarchical community would do well to try to smooth out the big ups and downs from year to year so as to keep the differential rewards in line with instituted status.

Let us compare the appropriate cosmologies that are likely to develop in two contrasted types of social organization. (1) Consider the community whose members want to strengthen community bonds—the heavier the commitment to solidarity, the more the reluctance to foment internal conflict. Community is always fragile; members will need to exhort one another to submit their individual desires to community control if they want to prevent the group from falling apart. So they will remind themselves of their ancestors and their proud traditions. Let us suppose that to reduce fratricidal strife, they have instituted sharply defined separations and buffered their subunits within a hierarchy, closing the community itself against the outside. Such a community

61

will prefer not to allow deviants and misfits to become the occasion of divisive feuding or to allow authority to be challenged. It will seek to reduce political discussion.

It will prefer to allocate responsibility for disaster to the victims and their kin. In such a community the strategy of blame-stopping makes the whole cosmos morally sensitive: Every little pain and loss will be reckoned a well-aimed rebuke, every crop failure or drought a punishment. Perhaps the pressure to deflect blaming and to stop its spread would produce an unacceptable load of guilt impossible to bear. So the same community will create machineries of expiation. The result is the morally punitive and conciliatory cosmos: a neat social invention, most richly developed within a context of religion.

(2) In contrast to the way a moralized cosmos serves the purpose of a hierarchical community, consider the society with a strong commitment to individual enterprise and fair competition. For such an adversarially minded people, the view that nature punishes members for their internal strife will not do at all. They are founding their social institutions on internal conflict. When everyone sees confrontation as the condition of justice, they are ready to see giant leaders ermerge, collect followings, challenge their rivals, and clash in public showdowns that will temporarily define power and precedence. This is a radically different kind of society, resting on a different pattern of social values.

For this scenario to be successively renewed, a neutral cosmos will do best. Nature has to be free of moral bias: Instead of a single commitment to community, natural forces will be divisible so as to work for different contestants. A variety of morally neutral forces can be captured by individuals and enrolled in their service. The more individualistically competitive the society, the more the usual toll of misfortunes will be attributed to a rival's fortunate destiny from birth, to his secret resources, or to sheer luck elevated as a cosmic explanatory principle. So far from avoiding the spirit of factionalism, inquiry into the causes of disaster is allowed to inflame it. The successful star is always tempted to call a stop to the fierce competition and perhaps to institutionalize either a bureaucracy or an aristocracy around himself and his heirs. But others keep the system fluid by the strategy of open confrontation: Appropriate explanations of disasters make room for new stars to rise—better secrets, talent, holiness, or luck on his side; and when X starts to fail, the same theory allows his supporters to drift away, saying that his technology has run down, his demon has deserted him, or his luck has run out. Instead of seeking to blame, there is seeking to claim responsibility for what has happened, as do political terrorists. Each actor, pursuing his private ends, is busily joining or leaving coalitions: Unsuccessful operations get driven down and out of the market; the few big ones emerge for a period of glory. The cosmology sustains something like a box-office register of superstar success. It justifies the changes in alignment that everyone needs to be ready to make. There is a large anthropological literature on the subject of superstar cosmology. The most original and clear account of this process describes how claims to *baraka* or holiness are validated in an Islamic society (Gellner 1969).

Now a strong contrast has emerged. When practical wisdom dictates band-wagoning as the best policy, the outcome of any confrontation justifies switching from one leader to another. Whereas in the moralized hierarchical cosmos, nature stays whole and steadfast to her loyal followers, in the adversarial culture, the various decisive fragments of nature are fickle. The culturally different attitudes to risks are but part and parcel of distinctive social arrangements.

In modern industrial society, the inspectorate is professionally specialized for anticipating danger. A new literature is emerging which shows how very differently its role is conceived and carried out in America (more adversarial and public, operating with fixed nationwide preventive regulations) and in Britain (more shared community between inspector and producer, more flexible rules, more cost-sensitive and locally adapted regulations).

Inspectorate

The Kemeny report on the accident at Three Mile Island (1979) notes that no office within the NRC specifically examines the interface between human beings and machines. At the same time, it clearly assumes that this interface is an organizational problem of efficiency and control (pp. 53, 55). However, an inspectorate is very much influenced by cultural bias in the larger society which appoints it. Indeed, two quite different discourses on the style and duties of the inspectorate can be discerned in the United Kingdom and the United States. Eric Ashby, on behalf of the former, prefers a pragmatic mode which has evolved over two centuries, and which can best be designated by what it is not—a nonpolicy, a nonadversarial style, nonuniversalistic, nonpreventative, noncoercive—a peculiarly benign system from which "impracticable ideas have been eliminated" (Ashby and Anderson 1981:153). Some doubts about how effective this system is have been expressed (O'Riordan 1982:9), but that there are two distinct inspectorate traditions is widely attested (Vogel 1980). The American discourse is about fairness, cost-effectiveness, efficiency, coercion, prevention of collusion (Crandall and Lave 1981). If each inspectorate tradition is deeply embedded in cultural values, the question of relative efficiency gives way to the question of whether one mode could be successfully transferred to another culture. The research would need to compare other, constitutional structures and safeguards (see Douglas 1983) if it is not to end up with a reverent salute to mystic cultural values. Stigler (1975), while questioning the cost-effectiveness of regulatory agencies, has laid down some guidelines for a more modest comparative study.

These various procedures correspond directly to differences in culture. The calls for showdown or cover up respond to deep commitments to how the good society should be.

Two kinds of society, each with its distinctive cosmology of blame have been used so far to illustrate cultural analysis of risk perception. The adversarial society on the one hand, and the hierarchical society on the other have been picked because they correspond so well with the currently long-entrenched typologizing about society. (See chapter 8.) Reflection on this general problem requires a basis for comparing human societies that will not be distorted by differences in technological power, literacy, scale, length of known traditions, and so on, but will work as well to reveal patterns of values in a family or tribe, factory or office.

Summary: This chapter broaches the issue of credibility, rumor transmission, and the social control of information.

According to research on public perception of risks, people regularly underestimate risks in familiar situations and low-probability risks. They get worried by media-reported events that seem dramatic (air crashes with film stars on board) and less worried by undramatic losses (such as deaths from asthma).

Salience

"Salience" makes one interpretation more available than another (Tversky and Kahneman 1974). Different kinds of salience are used to explain the variations in perception between different communities or different times. The references to salience are valuable as attempts to differentiate perceptual processes, but since they do not reach the culturally learnt coding which provides principles of selectivity and attention, they can only serve to signal discrepancies between expert and public views (Slovic, Lichtenstein, and Fischhoff 1979).

The media give "salience" to large-scale disasters from recent tornadoes and earthquakes, but presumably salience and recency eventually fade into the familiar background. This is what one

65

would expect, but Lawless's study (1974), reported in Kates (1978), shows increasing public concern tending to narrow the gap between media reports of technological risks and official responsiveness. The media and lobbies work hard to get "salience."

> An example of the politicized use of worst-case scenarios is a recent letter sent out by the Union of Concerned Scientists which contains the following statements: "These are the facts: one accident from one plant could kill as many as 45,000 people, cause $17 billion in property damage, and contaminate an area the size of Pennsylvania." Notice that no mention is made of the minuscule probabilities assigned to this worst case scenario by those who developed it. [Slovic, Lichtenstein, and Fischhoff 1979]

Our first question about perception of risk is why so many in their layman's role judge everyday hazards to be safe and think themselves able to cope when they cannot. A common-sense view of risk makes no puzzle about this. The common-sense view sets the individual in a social context of interdependent fellow beings who offer and withdraw support: A reputation for recklessness, meanness, craziness, or cowardice will destroy the individual's chances of community help. If a group of individuals ignore some manifest risks, it must be because their social network encourages them to do so. Their social interaction presumably does a large part of perceptual coding on risks.

The Risky Shift

> One sustained attempt to predict the effect of the social group on attitudes to risk should here be summarized. While testing the conformity hypothesis, some social psychologists noticed that the data provided some evidence for a contrary hypothesis—risky shift—suggesting that groups make riskier decisions than individuals (Stoner 1961; Nordhoy 1962). Social psychologists pursued this hypothesis with great enthusiasm until 1971. Since then an increasing number of scholars have questioned the risky shift literature both on conceptual and methodological grounds (Myers and Lamm 1976). Now there seems to be a consensus that the phenomenon has little to do with risk per se; the risky-shift research is now re-labeled as "group choice shifts" or "group polarization of attitudes." Most of the studies used a design called the Choice Dilemmas Questionnaire (CDQ). For a description of CDQ see Wallach, Kogen, and Bem (1962). For an alternative methodology involving gambling studies see Zajonc et al. (1968). A number of theories have been advanced to explain the risky-shift phenome-

non. The risk-as-value theory argues that there is a cultural value attached to risk-taking (Brown 1965). Individuals assume that they uphold the cultural values more successfully than others do; when they in fact discover that their choices are not as risky as those of others, they shift in the direction of greater risk. For variants of this theory see Pruitt (1971) and Fraser et al. (1970). For an empirical test of the risk-as-value theory, see Carlson and Davis (1971). An alternative theory attempting to explain risky shift could be labeled the *diffusion of responsibility* theory. It argues that groups tend to make riskier decisions than individuals because there is someone with whom to share the responsibility for the decision (Wallach, Kogan, and Bem 1974). For variants of this theory see Dion, Baren, and Miller (1971).

Expert risk analysis takes as its decision-making unit the individual agent, excluding from the choice any moral or political feedback that he may be receiving from his surrounding society. The rational agent of theory is deculturated. Common sense expects all choosing and deciding to be done with consultation. The rational agent of common sense is a being whose values and choices are embedded in a particular culture. For a well-nuanced statement of this view of culture, see Alexander (1979) for whom culture in evolutionary terms means

> the central aspect of the environment into which every person is born and must succeed or fail, developed gradually by the collection of humans that have preceded us in history, and with an inertia refractory to the wishes of individuals. . . . The striving of individuals would be to *use* culture, not necessarily by changing it, to further their own reproduction. . . . It would not matter if one were a legislator *making* laws, a judge *interpreting* them, a policeman *enforcing* them, a lawyer *using* them, a citizen *obeying* them, a criminal *circumventing* them, each of the behaviors can be seen as a particular strategy within societies governed by law. . . .

Actively invoked conventional wisdom is the sense in which I shall be using the word "culture." Since it is apt to be elevated (as in high culture) or downgraded as a residual explanation (as when rational motives seem inadequate) an unmystified account of culture will help at the outset of this argument. Culture is the publicly shared collection of principles and values used at any one time to justify behavior. Human behavior itself being channeled in public institutions, the principles and values uphold the forms of institutional life. Since this life takes place in a given environment, with given physical resources and techniques of exploitation and political pressures, the culture of a time and place speaks for the current solutions to political and environmental issues. In a strong sense, it represents the multiple cost-benefit analyses which balance all individuals' interests as agents dependent on the decisions of others. In this sense, the word "culture" corresponds to the individual's sense of social environment, at once adversarial and supporting, in which he has to fight for his interests and fight on behalf of the community and in the name of the community.

So culture represents the well-known sense of consultation and negotiation at every important turning point, as well as the sense of being provided with smoothly rubbed grooves of habit down which the uncontroversial issues can be dispatched. Culture would seem to be the coding principle by which hazards are recognized. The cultural standards of what constitute appropriate and improper risks emerge as part of the assignment of responsibility. They are fundamental to social life. When asked about the risks he takes, an individual has to make his answer start from some culturally established norm of due carefulness. So a daring mountaineer will rather boast of how he refused to budge when certain bad weather signs appeared; an Olympic skier will rather boast of his care of equipment. Both, denying that they take risks, assert that they avoid silly risks. Military leaders have to take risks for the men under their command after years of hearing recitals of famous battles; they know about possible ostracism for a misjudgment that costs lives or even court martial if they have been cowardly or rash (Keagan 1976). Every sick person knows that the sick role involves consultation among friends, and accepting their advice or being ready to defy their anger if illness worsens and the advice has not been followed. Decisions about which practitioner or which regime to follow are subject to community criticism.

Perceptions of Sickness

The perception of risk in everyday life parallels the perception of health and is likely to be as closely controlled by standardized perceptions of coping ability, responsibility, and reciprocity. In medical sociology there is relevant work on the social processes which code who should be consulted among family and neighbors, who should be selected as physician, and the sources of authority and the credibility of the latter. The individual who adopts a sick role finds himself a member of a therapeutic community, and the advice he gets depends on its network characteristics (Boswell 1969; Henderson, 1935; Jantzen 1978; Fox 1980).

The most inveterate gamblers repudiate the reproach of risk-taking, and insist that they are not playing with luck but skill.

Gambling

Gamblers claim to respect skill in their fellow gamblers more than size of winnings. Research in Britain shows that regular players in various games of chance claim that skill, not luck explains the patterns of success (Downes 1976; Zola 1964).

The more isolated a person, the weaker and more dispersed is his social network, the less his decisions are subject to public scrutiny, and the more he sets his own norms of reasonable risk. But as soon as there is a community, the norms of acceptability are debated and socially established. This activity constitutes the definitional basis of community.

A community uses its shared, accumulated experience to determine which foreseeable losses are most probable, which probable losses will be most harmful, and which harms may be preventible. A community also sets up the actors' model of the world and its scale of values by which different consequences are reckoned grave or trivial.

Reasonable Casualties

Wilderness survival courses are organized by Outward Bound, which aims at building individual "self-confidence and skills through stressful physical challenge." Between 1971 and 1979 twelve people died while participating in the program. In 1978 three participants died while kayaking in a storm off the west coast of Mexico. The parents of two victims charged Outward Bound with negligence and have filed law suits demanding $1 million each. The parents of another woman who died while participating in an Outward Bound mountain-climbing course in 1977 have initiated a law suit against Outward Bound demanding $2.5 million (New York *Times*, November 15, 1979; *Newsweek*, December 3, 1979; Washington Post, November 23, 1979).

Presumably, kids are sent to adventure schools to learn how to cope. It would be very interesting to know why the outcry against conditions with high probability of disaster was so delayed. Are twelve deaths of students of wilderness survival courses in eight years to be seen as a reasonable level of casualties? Who are the people who sue for $2.5 million damages for the loss of a daughter in a climbing course, and who are the other bereaved parents who have signed in advance that they will not sue at all?

Victims of Crime

Studies on perceived dangers of crime suggest that there are simple features of the social network that affect fear, suspicion, and the expectation of being able to cope. In general, potential victims of crime have a sound perception of the risks they run. Low income sections and black populations are both more exposed to crime and are also accurate in their awareness of this risk. Women and elderly people tend to exaggerate their vulnerability to crime. This is explainable by cultural factors: Women tend to be socialized into high-risk awareness; they are trained to expect attack; elderly people are isolated and their sense of danger corresponds to their weak sense of social support. The low correlation between facts and fears among the women and the elderly may be precisely the result of their cultivated fortress mentality. Their lower vulnerability (compared with their expectations) is due to the very success of the precautions they take to protect themselves (Garofalo 1979; Balkin 1979).

To trace common-sense ideas about norms for acceptable risks, surely some research would test correlations between community strength and the accuracy of individual members' assessments of risks. The most suggestive work on these lines has been focused on rumor and the social conditions for correctly receiving or for distorting information.

Rumor

According to Buckner (1965), the important studies on rumor transmission come to contradictory conclusions. Rumors (unconfirmed messages that pass from person to person) are thought either to snowball or to lose fuzzy detail and wild elaborations in the process of transmission. The panic that gripped Orleans in 1969 because of rumors of a sinister Jewish conspiracy to deliver girls to white-slave dealers (Morin 1971) is a case of snowballing. The rumor became a full-blown anti-Semitic myth, propagated by middle-class Catholic matrons and girls, expressing, according to Morin, a collective civic anxiety about modernism and the erosion of regional culture. Caplow's theory (1947) is that the formation of definite channels along which rumors are transmitted

70

increases their diffusion and veracity: in wartime increasing negative prestige attached to the transmission of false rumors; the
population developed increasing scepticism, and demand for objectivity led to drawing of a sharp line between rumors and other information; rumors were labeled as such in the telling and names of
sources were attached to doubtful statements. Buckner's research
called attention to variations in the development of rumors according to the interconnectedness of their bearers' social networks.
Both imply a link between regular interconnectedness and trust-
worthiness (Allport and Postman 1947). The credibility of experts
is often questioned because of suspected vested interests; the extent to which people feel they have been lied to in the past is said
to affect public perceptions of nuclear technology. (See Piehler et
al. 1974). The importance of this subject is signaled by Sen's account (1977) of the dire effects of rumor on food supplies during
the Bengal famine of 1943.

The topic of social control of information is surely due for renewed attention. In 1962 James Coleman referred to earlier studies on gregariousness (sociability) and group membership as having an effect on the flow of information: "the literature on
primary groups . . . emphasizes the importance of the group in
moulding the view of the world and sanctioning the actions of individual members" (Coleman et al. 1962). Already, back in 1948,
Leon Festinger had written: "There would seem to be a sufficient
accumulation of studies to show that social relationships are important factors in the flow of information, but very little evidence
on what kinds of social relationships make what kind of difference" (Festinger et al. 1948). That old research lacked focus.
When it is revived it can now find a powerful focus in the question of public credence to rumors about risks from technology.
    The same may be said about the research on subjective compe-
tence. This concept was proposed by Almond and Verba (1963,
1980) in their important analysis of political cultures. It seems to
be equivalent at a different level of social organization to the phenomenon of subjective immunity to risk. Subjective competence
means that, quite independently of objective criteria, some political cultures generate in the populace a sense that they are capable of influencing political decisions. Whether the confidence is
justified or not, Almond and Verba believed it to be a necessary
ingredient for stable democracy. Psychologists will be tempted to
trace the sense of subjective immunity to psychological factors.
But the research on its political counterpart suggests we should
find its sources in social organization.

71

The common-sense view of risk is to be gleaned from everyday conversations, precautions taken, and excuses made. Underlying it is a concept of responsibility. The rational agent stands at the bar of public criticism in his own community as a responsible, moral person. The cultural coding of responsibility is also the coding for perceiving risks.

Summary: This chapter traces one line of development in the theory of choice that follows Simon's work on bounded rationality. He drew attention to the enormous intellectual complexity of decision-making assumed by the theory. By substituting "satisficing" for maximizing he has been able to synthesize many observations of how decision units actually behave, assuming that they accept upper and lower thresholds of failure and success. Research in agricultural economics indicates how these limits are culturally defined.

Rational choice needs to take into account the working of a principle that sets the lower limit for acceptable risks. Utility theory allowed for outcomes being so undesirable as to fall outside of the individual's schedule of preferences. Engel's law (Houthakker 1957) recognizes a kind of safety-first concern. According to this observation, the poorer the households in a given income distribution, the lower is the elasticity of response to changes in the price of food. The household head has an order of spending that strives to ensure the basic requirements of his family. In investment analysis, liquidity preference is a similar idea, which, according to Hicks, entered economic discourse in the 1930s. An investment trust or discount house has liabilities that must be protected: "a worse than 'expected' outcome must be dreaded more than a better than expected outcome is desired—because of the impact which unfavorable outcomes may have on the non-liquid elements in the situation . . . hence the motive force for certainty" (Hicks 1962).

The simplest example of this concern to limit the worst outcomes is the practice usual among pastoralist tribes to divide a big herd of livestock among several dispersed herdsmen. It corresponds to Daniel Bernoulli's advice that it is advisable to divide goods which are exposed to some danger into several portions rather than to risk them all together (Bernoulli 1738: 30, par. 16).

Early attempts to understand behavior under uncertainty used the maximizing of expected gain as the main criterion of rationality. But some lower limit of tolerable loss was also recognized (Roy 1952).

The various bits and pieces of a general safety-first principle became formalized within Simon's concept of bounded rationality (1955). The ideas embodied in this paper were initially developed in 1952 (see Simon 1979:7), which puts it in the same short period as other famous questionings of rational choice theory (see chapter 4). In this decisive new development Simon starts with two reasons for questioning the adequacy of the theory of rational choice. One is the grotesquely powerful intellectual capacities which are supposedly called upon for every choice. The theory expects an impossibly complex analytic exercise from the rational agent. The other is the neglect of the rational agents' environment: "We must be prepared to accept the possibility that what we call the 'environment' may be, in part, within the skin of the biological organism." This is a useful approach to the fact that the individual's thinking apparatus, with its concepts and assessments of the world, though it may lie within his skin, is also part of his environment.

"Satisficing" is Simon's word for the method of simplifying complex choices, which he argues is more commonly used than the "maximizing" behavior assumed by utility theory. A satisficing firm sets its goals to the attaining of a certain level of profit, to holding a certain share of the market, or to keeping up a certain level of sales. Maximizing behavior does not put any limit on what may be achieved. Satisficing is adaptive behavior. In this approach, rational choice takes place within bounds whose upper and lower limits are set semi-independently. This is consistent with psychological studies of the formation and change of levels of aspiration. It is assumed that goals have some connection with what is attainable. In classical utility theory, the zero point in the scale of utility is set arbitrarily; in this approach, the adaptive aspiration level defines a zero point and a ceiling. Simon cites evidence that firms with a declining share of the market strive more vigorously than firms whose share in the market is steady or increasing. There is further evidence from peasant communities where a socially set standard of living defines upper and lower limits of striving (Sahlins 1974).

This hypothesis has inspired much empirical research on risk-taking. However, the clear implication that the levels of aspiration are to a large extent culturally standardized has not been worked through. How else could the floors and ceilings be set?

Should we have an air-cushion model of the personality according to which the total amount of risk-seeking is roughly the same? Then we could suppose that those who work in very steady occupations will release their natural propensities for risk-seeking by choosing dangerous leisure thrills—sky-diving, hang-gliding, or gambling. Rather than seeking violence in sports to compensate for placid work conditions, the contrary seems more plausible: that individuals in occupations that demand risk-taking should seek reinforcement in their leisure choices. Smith (1979) finds that his data intended to investigate the existence of a violent subculture point rather to occupational subcultures consistently extending professional criteria regarding the use of violence.

Or do some people carry from birth a psychological trait that biases them to choose risky sports as well as risky occupations? The personality bias might be genetic, like hair color or blood grouping, or it could be learned. Unfortunately, testing for the innate personality element is practically impossible. In thinking about risk-prone behavior, it is better to focus on the possible social influence than to try to eliminate it. When uncertainty is at a very high level and everyone is taking big risks, the cultural norms will encourage more risk-seeking. The comparison of the Virginian settlers with the East Coast Puritans in the seventeenth century illustrates this cultural response to an environment of uncertainty. As if contending with uncertainties of shipping and prices and the vagaries of the tobacco crop were not enough added to uncertainties caused by the high death rate of young men, instead of trying to reduce uncertainty, the Virginians invented more gambles with other stakes, gambling with horse-races, cards, and any outcomes that could be bet upon. The self-sufficient Puritan communities abhorred gambling and were risk averse (Breen and Innes 1980; Morgan 1975:395–432).

The state of the art in the social sciences provides no way of explaining why people climb Everest, why banks give financial support to what is the riskiest business. Climbing is an occupation in which the chances of a fatal accident are between one in eight and one in ten per expedition. Developing a cultural theory of risk-taking, Michael Thompson (1980) identifies two social structures that generate complementary, polarized attitudes toward risk. His cultural model is compatible with the psychological model of risk-taking and risk-averse personalities, while allowing for cultural reinforcements for initial choices. Cultural specialization in respect of risk creates economic benefits for each type. A risk-sharing strategy and a pessimistic world view that justifies the strategy go with a collective, communitarian social context with expectations that gains will be shared as well as losses. A risk-narrowing strategy ("Spot on he wins, way out he loses"), justified by an optimistic world view works in a society of individuals who are not expected to share gains or losses.

On this argument, each cultural pattern of risk is sustained by its own appropriate economic structure. There is good reason to suppose that most societies select and train certain members to take physical risks and reward them for doing so by heaping prestige on the successful adventurers. Human survival is at high risk in small-scale economies based on primitive technology. The community problem is often solved by risk-allocating institutions. Most hunters and gatherers combine a steady subsistence based on vegetable resources with unpredictable, irregular sources of wild game. Their nomadic pattern first assures the basic supplies, moving to pick up the various wild harvests as they ripen here and there. The steady tasks are allocated to women. At the same time, young men are trained to go off after the hazardous game on long treks, entailing hardship and danger. The same applies in more advanced technology, but the comparisons are difficult because of the variety of risks involved—career risks, income risks, and physical risks. A similar distribution of riskier and less risky sources of income is found at the household level in modern society: Academics earn a steady salary and treat writing as irregular income while many politicians treat journalism as a safety net should votes go wrong. Friedman (1957) has provided an analysis of how permanent and transitory sources of income on American farms are spread to reduce variance from year to year. This is consistent with investment behavior: A company that plans to stay in business spreads its assets among high and low-risk prospects. Attempting to secure an economic baseline is like the military commander's concern to protect his rear from attack.

Among farmers it is not immediately obvious what is the riskier of two crops. The subsistence crop is usually safe as to production, but if the farmer means to sell the surplus, food crop prices are notoriously fluctuating: If he has decided to allocate a large amount of land to, say, rice or corn and less to a profitable but risky cash crop, he may find that he has to take a loss on his farming year when he tries to sell the surplus rice or corn (Kunreuther and Wright 1979:214–18).

Most complex problems of management turn out to have solutions that are both technological and institutional. Effective performance needs optimal combinations of skills and resources. The deeper that agricultural economists delve into the farmer's decisions, and the more that is learned about his goals and constraints, the more he is revealed as a responsible agent, making defensible decisions which reveal a strong safety-first concern (Roumasset et al. 1979).

For example, the poor Indian farmers in Colombia described by Ortiz (1979:231–40) make a careful cash crop strategy, following the latest information about prices and techniques and the state of the market. The farmer does not find it difficult to decide what cash crop to plant and what capital investment to make, so these decisions can be made ahead of time. He has his own estimating procedures and formulae for evaluating outcomes. He has a concept of a tolerable loss—that is, an income which, though below normal receipts, does not fall below unavoidable expenses (loans to be replaced, marketing costs, seeds, fertilizers, wages, and a sum for needed consumer goods). The farmer does not conceptualize his activities within a single strategy with an annual income, but as a bunch of separate activities, each having its potential loss and gain points. Though he can work out the costs and profits of cash crops, his consumption needs pose a more difficult problem. In general, once the very basic subsistence requirements are ensured, these farmers are not afraid of some risk-taking. They vastly prefer risky cash crops to the security of selling labor time to a local planter (Ortiz 1979:243–44). Losing their claim to land seems to be the very worst disaster, to prevent which they design their safety-first strategies.

Empirical studies of economic decision-making in investment

77

analysis as well as in low-income farming ought to discourage psychologists from dividing the world into risk-seeking and risk-averse personalities. If circumstances change, when one strategy is unpromising, the same individual will adopt the other. But such flexible strategies are difficult to observe by means of attitude surveys. There seems to be a problem about developing theoretical ideas about economic risk-aversion and risk-taking in a real, live world context. For example, Howard Kunreuther, who has actually made an elegant historical demonstration of the safety-first model of farmers' decisions (1979), when designing a monumental survey of contemporary disaster insurance assumed that irrational home owners were bounding the scope of their concerns when they underestimated the likelihood of quakes or flood damage to their houses or failed to insure them (Kunreuther et al. 1978). In other words, Kunreuther and his colleagues fell back on pathology, when they needed to develop the model of rational choice to take account of culturally defined thresholds. Giving top priority to holding onto the family farm or ignoring particular risks is not necessarily irrational. In the whole pattern of perceived options it may be a good strategy for survival, equivalent to giving top priority to buying staple foods at another level of the domestic economy.

The economists assume that the critical level which the decision-maker tends to protect is set privately. However, the analysis is vastly improved if it is conceded that lower levels that define disaster (and upper levels that define overachievement) may be set communally. It makes more sense to understand them as culturally determined rather than as individual limits to economic behavior. The same models for explaining individual satisficing can do well for describing cultural conventions. Indeed, in default of evidence, many economists assume that individual utility preferences are common to the group being studied. This can easily be tested. If we know enough about crop yield and price variance and costs for a given community, we would be entitled to treat individual subjective preference as if it were cultural preference, still using the definition of culture as the accumulated experience of the society and its adaptation to the environment.

Simon has drawn attention to the inordinate intellectual difficulties faced by the individual decision-maker. What super individual can be clever enough to do the calculations? Who can hold all the options and their probable outcomes in mind long enough for the decision-making process to be followed? Generally, various heuristics or rules of thumb are used in place of the full calculation. Ortiz's Colombian farmers' practice of streaming separate activities, each with its potential gain and loss points, is a good accounting heuristic. It is widely assumed that these rules of thumb, though time-saving, are liable to introduce bias. However, this partly depends on how the problem is defined.

Heuristics

As simplifying procedures for teaching or learning devised in order to facilitate rapid treatment of complex problems, heuristics work by simplification. Inevitably, they are potential sources of distortion. This must be especially apparent when the problem being presented in a psychology test situation is treated heuristically by the experimental subject (Kahneman and Tversky 1973, 1974). In real life, one would like to suppose that a heuristic that is so distorting as to be counterproductive would be soon discarded. It could be helpful for one category of users and unhelpful for another. Lopes (1981) has pointed out that the comparative rigidity of decision sciences' use of utility-maximizing assumptions plus long-run interpretation is functional for insurance companies but not for low-income farmers for whom all risks are short-run risks—an example close to home of a heuristic that distorts the problem.

In a brief summary of the work on risk heuristics as a source of error, Otway and Thomas (1982) sound a pessimistic note: Recognizing that this strand of cognitive psychology has relevance for societal risk perception, they feel that the authors have missed the main point and ask how this work can in any way help to solve the political issues whose urgency initiated the research in the first place.

Two heuristics which have been identified as rather unreliable aids to assessing frequency and probability are "availability" and saliency. Any experience which makes a particular source of danger memorable, such as the mugging of a movie star or the automobile accident that kills a princess, or the most recent fire or flood, tends to displace the ordinary backgrounding treatment which news of earlier losses tend to receive. In the long run of actual probabilities, these heuristics distort true frequencies. But seen against the individual tendency to believe himself immune to damage afflicting other travelers or consumers, the salience and availability heuristics must have a corrective effect by enhancing awareness that is apt to be smothered by subjective immunity. Forcing each other to listen to news of horrible disasters is a cultural process that can help to remedy the individual's neglect of due precautions. The heuristic seems more dysfunctional in a short-range individualized test situation than in a long-range cultural perspective.

Heuristics are also conventions: By being shared within a community they resolve problems of coordination. In this capacity, they are the essential element of the cultural process. Not only do they aid in making risk assessments, but they enable each member of the community to predict what the others will do in a given context. Thus, they code and transmit market information. When all the members of the community live under the same constraints, they need to share flexible strategies for dealing with the varied environment and for agreeing on what is likely to happen. Gladwin (1975) has illustrated how the assessments of uncertain factors are coded by fish sellers in Ghana who categorize the state of demand into "good market," "spoiled market," "little fish," and "plentiful fish." With this categorization, plus knowledge of the suppliers' price for fish, they can calculate what their profit will be. See also Ortiz (1980) for a parallel analysis of planting decisions for a peasant farming community. It is not enough to treat heuristics as mere cognitive aids to the individual decision-maker. By clarifying options and establishing expectations they create some predictability and enable cultural values to be agreed. The work of anthropologists in agricultural economics (see Barlett 1980) makes an original contribution to understanding the cultural processes which reduce uncertainty.

One of the functions of the cultural process is to provide ready-made categories for storing and retrieving information; social pressures ensure that the various separate responsibilities will be remembered. The alleged difficulties of the cognitive exercise collapse as soon as culture is admitted to have a role. The farmer's wife, when she reminds her husband of priorities as to food, clothing, and shelter, is not only speaking for herself. She has her place to consider among her neighbors to whom she gives her fair share of criticism if they default on their social obligations. She has internalized the cultural categories of the women; her husband has internalized those of the men. Members of the same community know what happens to a family if it avoids the risks of farming its own land and goes for the apparent security of wage labor. They know the bad things that can happen to old people if the farm is sold. A shared culture tells them where they stand in the table of life chances, without elaborate calculations.

Perceptions of Life Chances

Dahrendorf (1979:29–32) has eloquently made the case for a life-chance approach to social justice. The calculations of relative opportunities that he proposes would both remedy the outsider's ignorance of local cultures (and indeed such statistics are used by governments and international agencies for those very purposes) and correct the naiveté of insiders (usually rather isolated ones) who really believe that every soldier can carry a field marshal's baton in his knapsack. But within a particular culture, knowledge of life chances is more reliably diffused, as Boltanski and others have shown: e.g., by questioning low-income mothers on their expectations for their children's educational and career achievements (Boltanski 1970). Culturally standardized expectations adjust individual's hopes to what is more probable. The process creates forms of salience in the flood of surrounding information and gives cues for what is to be regarded as normal and abnormal. Psychologists who are interested in "salience" of certain events and "availability" of certain kinds of interpretation in their effect on risk perception could do well to investigate standardized expectations in clearly defined communities.

The fortunes of the community around them vividly display in the lives of their friends consequences of too much risk-taking here or too much risk aversion there. The culture provides boundaries of rational economic choice as it defines the standard of living and the requirements of mutual aid. The living culture is the mnemonic system which holds the farmer to his priorities and leads him through what would be a horrendously difficult calculation were an individual to try to perform it on his own.

Modeling Cultural Behavior

Otway and Thomas (1982) thoughtfully remark that in contrast with the Bayesian statistician ". . . a Bayesian psychologist might well be interested in something other than an 'external' model of what people should do and the discrepancy between this and what they actually do. He might adopt a rather different perspective, trying instead to understand the behavior from the 'inside,' from the individual's point of view. And part of the exercise of building an 'internal' model would mean giving due weight to the ecology and purposes of judgments and choices in everyday life . . . the studies

81

which come closest to explaining (as opposed to describing) the so-called biases and irrationalities of lay publics are those which relate behavioral observations to wider processes whereby information is selected and integrated alongside representations of the world already held by the subject as a result of earlier experiences, and motivations ranging from preferences to life-directing goals." In other words, the focus should be shifted to modeling cultural influences on perception and choice.

This remarkable essay, whose first paragraph is headed "Confessions of Two Disillusioned Analysts," gives a fair and critical survey of the limitations and strengths of psychometric methods of analysis of perception. At this point, when it seems clear that cognitive psychology can only develop by joining issue with cultural processes, the problems of method should not seem invincible. The gross statistics of movements of prices which form the subject matter of economic theories of consumption are also gross indicators of movements of choice and tastes. They are not divorced either from individual cognitive or from cultural processes. The analyses of the tree-like structure of demand is essentially analogous (on a large public scale) to the analysis of individual decision-trees. Leontiev (1947) is especially good on the history of utility theory in showing how the concept of the rational individual agent applies to the large patterns of national consumption. What is most conspicuously difficult is to persuade the two sets of analysts that there is a mediating element, culture, which is worthy of their combined attention (Douglas and Isherwood 1978).

The question of acceptable standards of risk is part of the question of acceptable standards of living and acceptable standards of morality and decency, and there is no way of talking seriously about the risk aspect while evading the task of analyzing the cultural system in which the other standards are formed.

Summary: This chapter scans the literature for typologies of organizations that might influence perceptions of risk. In the theory of organizations, the question of how different types of social environment affect decision-making has been raised, but it has never been held in focus.

"The organizational and social environment in which the decision maker finds himself determines what consequences he will anticipate, what ones he will ignore. In a theory of organization, these variables cannot be treated as unexplained, independent factors, but must be determined and explained by the theory" (March and Simon 1958). It was a long time ago that this was said by March and Simon. It suggests that organizational theory would have much to reveal about the rational agent's definition of a situation and selection of odds. There has indeed been considerable work on the differences of viewpoint from different parts of an organization, the worm's-eye view, the bird's-eye view, the leader's view, the outsider's view, the view from the workshop floor. Yet, in spite of this good sociological starting point, questions about human perception of risk are not traced to the qualitatively different characteristics of institutions. If it is conceded that institutions play any role, then it would follow that much of the inquiry about risk perception has been applied to the wrong units, to individuals instead of to institutions. The upshot of research on cultural bias even suggests that individuals do not try to make independent choices, especially about big political issues. Some policy aspects of this argument have been developed in Douglas and Wildavsky (1982). When faced with estimating the credibility of sources, values, and probabilities, they come already primed with culturally learned assumptions and weightings. This does not imply a deterministic influence on individuals. One could say that they have been fabricating their prejudices as part of the work of designing their institutions. They have set up their institutions as decision processors which shut out some options and put others in favorable light. The first choices before individuals lie between joining and not joining institutions of different kinds. At the next level individuals engage in continuous monitoring of their chosen institutional machinery. The big choices reach them in the form of questions of whether to reinforce authority or to subvert it, whether to block or to enable action. This is where rationality is exerted.

To understand rational behavior, we should examine this everyday monitoring process. It consists of applying two kinds of coherence tests to the institutional structure. One is the matching of promises to performance. For instance, the firm promises that jobs are safe, then someone gets fired; what are the probabilities that the firm's guarantees of security are reliable? The other test is applied to the principles of justification: Is their logic strong? What are the principles of classification? Are the rules contradictory? How coherent is the whole system of rules by which the institution works? Mishaps, misfortunes, threats, and disasters provoke the endless challenges and cogitation about the structure of institutional life. It is not difficult to see that this monitoring process establishes for any institution at the appropriate level some agreed norms for acceptable and unacceptable risk.

The central method of monitoring is to fasten attention on misfortunes.

Focus on Misfortune

"The test of what is the dominant motif is usually, perhaps always, to what a people attribute dangers and sickness and other misfortunes and what steps they take to avoid or eliminate them" (Evans-Pritchard 1956:315). For seeking the principles which focus attention on risks this is a better prescription than studying the smooth runs and sunny moments.

84

Evans-Pritchard (1937) defined this approach when he demonstrated that neither questions nor attributions of blame fall in random patterns of accusations, as would be the case if attribution were a function of the individual perceiver.

Any major mishap in an organization sparks off questions about responsibility. If the organization has been established long enough to have taken a particular form, the questions are not going to be random. Still less will the answers seem credible unless they reinforce the members' concerns about the form of the organization they live in. For example, if people in an organization dislike the way that top authority has been exercised, it will be credible that the responsibility for accidents be pinned at the top; in the course of being made answerable, the harshness and arbitrary weight of authority will be investigated and criticized. In the reverse direction of concern, if the majority are worried about the disruptive behavior of junior members in an organization and fearful of a possible challenge to traditional authority, then minor and major misfortunes will seem very plausibly to have been caused by the young Turks. This is compatible with attribution theory, extended beyond individuals to the life of institutions. It is important to recognize that the inquiries following on misfortune which focus on institutional norms and values represent the normal exercise of individual rational thought. Everyone is acutely concerned to hear the excuses and justifications for harm that has happened and to pass judgment. But they are not inquiring dispassionately. They bring to their tests of logical coherence culturally loaded intuitions about what the ideal organization ought to be, influenced by their memory of past investigations and precedents. Whether the institution has been developing in one direction or in another, the search for a culpable agent will be biased accordingly. This is how disasters, defined as either man-made or natural, become enmeshed with the micro-politics of institutions. Processes of blame-pinning or exonerating from blame strengthen the pattern of the organization and are actually an integral part of it. It is argued that the objectors to the Windscale nuclear plant, even though they failed to get the decision they sought, by their efforts changed the processes of accountability (Williams 1980:317).

Organization theory is poor in explanations of institutional blindness. The issue is rarely discussed and the actual typologies that emerge in a well-developed way are suprisingly few. A num-

85

ber of incipient typologies fragment and get lost. One popular contrast distinguishes large from small organizations, implying also that the large are complex and the small are simple. This never develops very far, because the small organizations quickly get discarded from the exercise. Organization theory seems unduly obsessed by the idea that problems are created by increase in scale.

Scale Effects

Sociology entertains a sentimental bias toward believing smallness of scale is better for effective political action, leadership, and decisions and that consequently the most significant organizational problems stem from increase in scale. For an influential statement, read Homans (1950). The measurement of economies and diseconomies of scale carries the implication for economic theory that for any particular situation a correct scale of operations can be identified. Economists could be expected to have the opposite bias from the sociologists, since their theory rests on the axiom that markets are only efficient when the number of sellers is large enough to prevent collusion. For a summary of the difference between economists' and political scientists' assumptions on this score, see Barry and Hardin (1982:39–50) introducing Olson's theory of collective action. Olson explicitly bases his theory on scale differences: "unless the number of individuals in a group is quite small . . ." and "the larger the group is, the further it will fall short . . . ," drawing quite explicitly on Homans' essentially romantic notion that small-scale, face-to-face social units are in themselves immune to the troubles that beset large organizations (1965). These implicit feelings about the relative ease of small-scale human co-operation have been challenged by Barry and Hardin (1982:25–26) and by Chamberlain (1982), concluding that scale effects are much more complex than is usually allowed.

It is worth noting that the social scientists' more vigorous concern for effects of scale is new compared with the biologists' well-established principles of allometry (Naroll and Von Bertalanffy 1956).

One definition of complexity distinguishes a system which has many parts from a simple system having only a few (La Porte 1975). This by implication links complexity to increasing scale. Another approach to complexity which depends on the combination of variety with logical entailment gives a very different classification of complex and simple systems, without implying anything about sheer number of constituent elements, or about prospects of collapse (Douglas and Gross 1981; Douglas 1984).

The prejudice may be enhanced by the fact that the large organizations can employ decision analysts as consultants, and so by default small organizations may seem to have few problems. Furthermore, sociologists tend to idealize the small, face-to-face forms of society. They assume that complexity is only a function of scale: Increase in scale leads to devolution, centralization, compartmentalization, and these lead to overloaded channels and problematical communications. While this is true, it is not the case that very small organizations do not have very grave problems that lead to factions, fission, and fizzling out. Smallness of scale is compatible with a high degree of internal complexity, devolution, and compartmentalization. An anthropological basis for social comparison needs to discount some of the effects of scale and to allow for the endemic problems of different kinds of social organization.

Principles of sociological classification derived from Max Weber provide slightly overlapping typologies. The contrast between charismatic leadership and routinized procedures, based on the distinctive roles of prophet and priest, has haunted much of Western social thought. But is it the leader who has charisma, or is it thrust upon the leader in certain kinds of political regimes? Contrasted leadership styles would be useful to the present purpose if the literature on charisma (whether on party leaders or on personality cults) did not tend too much to treat the leaders apart from the analysis of political regimes (Wildavsky 1984).

The other classificatory principle which dominates our thinking about society gives the contrast between market and bureaucratic rationality. Whereas routinization tends to lead to bureaucracy, charisma tends to float outside of both market and bureaucracy, giving us the illusion of three types. Whereas if charisma studies were well-integrated with leadership and interest-group studies, it might well appear that we only have identified two types: bureaucracy on the one hand, with its procedural rules and hierarchical values, and market on the other, dominated by means-end rationality. Certain developmental phases of either type develop scope for charismatic leaders to build fragile coalitions and bring them up to climax and predictable collapse. Direct focus on institutional constraints on perception is rare in the sociological literature.

Institutional Constraints on Perception

Engineers and public health officials have been compared in order to assess the viewpoint of professionals in government and industry. The concern of the public health official about environmental quality tends to decline with number of years in the profession. Both for engineers and public health officials, seniority brings increasing dedication to the agency, but the engineers perceive a wider range of problems facing society. Such comparisons point to how institutional effects on perception of risk could be investigated (Sewell 1971, 1973).

The paradigmatic centrality of these two types—bureaucracy and market—explains why it is so difficult to transfer to modern society any insights whatever from anthropology. Market is the fundamental condition of industrial society. And bureaucracy is seen as the development (unwanted, maybe) of high culture. Combined, they are the point of reference which separates types of modern society from those technologically simple ones studied by anthropologists. To bridge that impressive divide, a typology is needed that works at a higher level of generalization, allowing distinctive social forms to be seen apart from the accidents of literacy and technology. The typologizing effort in organization theory has largely been dominated by decision analysis. Here we find a formidable literature that assumes that kinds of thinking are related to kinds of organization. It is not surprising that only two kinds of decision-making are generally considered. The seminal article that sets the terms for the comparisons still being made is Lindblom's criticism (1959) of decision and organization theory (Lindblom 1965, 1979; Knott 1982). Here he contrasts Root style of decision-making which is rational, theoretical, and scientific with Branch style which is pragmatic, strategic, and incremental.

Much subsequent research inspired by this contrast has produced variations on the same basic distinction: synoptic contrasted with strategic policy programming, comprehensive budgeting versus incremental budgeting (Wildavsky 1975), cogitative and interactive kinds of policy formation. The theorizing shifts between different operational levels, between processes and their products, between different kinds of organization. But we always have two types of decision-making: the one strong on grand theory, the other weak on theory but relying successfully on social interaction to supplement its other lacks.

Several thinkers have tried to propose a third type of decision-making but failed to produce a coherent typology. Allison (1971) offers three models of government decision-making; the first is based on the individual behaving according to classical utility theory; the government is presented as if it were a single rational agent, able to know and rank its goals and solve its problems according to a rational appraisal of costs and benefits; the second echoes Lindblom's descriptions of actual organizational muddling through, contrary to the behests of theorists, with heavy recourse to fixed plans and routines. Allison's third model is a more complicated version of the utility theory used for his Model 1, in which the whole market of individual agents are bargaining, compromising, and making coalitions. In effect, instead of providing three distinct types, Allison is working with the usual two basic models—market and bureaucracy and bureaucracy seen from the inside as a market.

Steinbruner (1976) tries to have three models of cognition in organizations: a classic utility model (which corresponds roughly to Lindblom's rational comprehensive Root style of policy formulation), which he calls analytic thinking; a pragmatic interactive model, which corresponds to Lindblom's other model); a cybernetic model with bureaucratically restricted focus, which has much in common with the emphasis on fixed goals and operating procedures in Allison's Model 2. Again, the claim to have defined more than two basic types is not convincingly worked out. Both Steinbruner and Allison are interested in the central problem of how the prior mental set affects interpretations of events. Both imply that the mental set and its assumptions come from somewhere outside the analysis, perhaps from national culture or individual psychological makeup, whereas, according to the anthropological argument the individual makes an initial choice for a kind of organization and this commitment itself generates the decision-making and perceptual bias.

Moral Commitment

Ouchi (1980) has suggested a third organizational form from within this conceptual scheme. He calls "clan" a structure in which a total congruence of goals allows for much more informality and a less explicit statement of rules. But alas, an uncritical enthusiasm for the small in scale defeats the scheme. Ouchi sees the clan as emerging in response to failure of bureaucratic organization. He uses the argument from scale to claim that clans do not require explicit auditing and evaluation, because of the subtle, mutual monitoring of intimate coworkers. Like Rosabeth Moss

Kanter (1972), he assumes that moral commitment to common goals is an independent factor. If he can assume that moral commitment arises so easily, just from disappointment with the workings of bureaucracy, why can we not also suppose it to precede market relations and so reverse his argument? Both skip out of the central dilemma of political theory in which the issue over the centuries has been how shared moral commitment ever emerges and how it is sustained.

Given the central use of the idea of rational behavior in the theory of organization, one would expect the differences between the individual decision-maker and the organization to be fully spelled out. A recent review shows that the paradigmatic scheme of the organization seen as an individual is full of loose ends and not at all as well understood as one might expect of a central tool in decision theory. The two incomplete models which prevail treat the organization either as an individual within a market environment or as a market in which its constituent parts are individuals (Hogarth 1981).

A serviceable anthropological approach to organization searches for how the organization develops specific mechanisms of accountability and blame allocation. The commitment of individuals to these mechanisms produces an internal cost structure to which rational behavior must adapt if a particular individual within the organization is to do well. The whole organization must be well adapted to the structure of costs and benefits in the external environment if it is to survive. These adaptations are made by appeals to cosmological ideas which code the latent dangers in the universe so as to meet the institutional demand for coherence. Every member of an organization is monitoring his fellows' behavior by tests of accountability and coherence in the face of nature's pressures. The line that divides man-made from natural calamity is drawn in response to moral scrutiny of what is a reasonable level of performance. To learn the institutional blinders on perception, we need to consider how disasters get to be interpreted so as to fulfill individuals' purposes as they make moral demands on one another and as they set up institutional channels for their expectations to be realized. We will need a richer typology, more than two types of organization, and some good theory to link up the appeals to nature, the perceptions of risk, and the micro-politics of institutions.

Chapter 9   Risks Encoded

Summary: This concluding chapter extends some recent work on institutional economics to encoding of decisions within the structure of organizations. The individual takes a middle-range and short-range view of probabilities. Institutions carry perception into the long term. Different institutions vary the focus and constitute for individual members a differentiated experience of real world probabilities.

This volume pivots on a central contrast. On the one hand, the analysis of risk within the theory of choice, as we saw in chapter 4, clears away all adhering real world considerations; understandably, a pure theory of risk separates its topic from prejudices entertained by the decision-maker and from institutional and historical contingencies. On the other hand, in the real world the perception of probable natural losses is freighted with moral associations and institutional bias (as we saw in chapter 5). Here is constituted a practical dilemma for the social sciences. The current challenge to them concerns levels of risk acceptability. Such an issue cannot be discussed except in a context of moral and political theory. An anthropological approach combines an analysis of rational behavior with an account of the ethical constructs which are used for focusing social issues. But anthropology is a fringy, primitive form of discourse. It is not axiomatized. It has no core of established propositions. On its own it can never correct the focus gone awry. We may try to make the case for an anthropological approach by borrowing from economists and rational choice theorists to make a joint approach to the central puzzle of risk perception.

91

The problem that initially called forth a new subdiscipline of risk perception had to do with extraordinary sources of danger. The industrial use of nuclear power introduces the idea of gravely damaging effects following on very low probability events. Since it seems that human cognition normally works with a focus on medium probabilities, these dangers could be presumed to fall beyond the lay public's cognitive threshold. Yet the initial question was the other way: Some members of the lay public were deeply concerned about such events and the experts were saying that the concern was unnecessary. We also saw that the possibility of attributing blame draws and holds individual attention. We saw that a strong sense of moral outrage could be enough to focus individual attention to dangers beyond the close-bounded range of cognition. From this it has seemed to some that being forced involuntarily to assume heavy risks would account for the political alertness of the public to risks from industry. From here the line between natural and man-made disasters has seemed to be the direct key to understanding hostility to nuclear power and to toxic industrial chemicals—clear cases in which human responsibility can be located. But exploitation does not always produce political alertness. The sense of being exploited is not an independent variable. This explanation does not help to explain passivity in many Western societies and in Japan to nuclear power being developed for peaceful purposes. That line between man-made and natural causes is masqueraded as one of the neutral divisions of the universe so that it can be used as a measure of personal accountability in the here and now. Instead of treating nature uncritically as given, we should ask what social factors sometimes carry attention beyond the normal perceptual focus on medium-frequency events.

The argument to be developed is that the institutional filter through which risks are perceived imposes a consistent distortion upon the probabilities. To say that the institutional lens obscures the risk issues is partly true. It also uses the risk issues to clarify another set of problems. It is more illuminating to regard the risks as a lens for sharpening the focus on the social organization itself. Institutions use the risk issue to control uncertainty about human behavior, to reinforce norms, and to facilitate coordination.

In this argument, the steps have been cut out by workers acknowledging a particular debt to Herbert Simon. We saw his influence on the analysis of safety-first responses to risks (in chapter 7). His second criticism of the unbounded rationality assumptions of the theory of choice was its neglect of the total system or environment in which the rational agent makes choices. What follows is an extension of his idea that "what we call the 'environment' may be, in part, within the skin of the biological organism" (Simon 1955). In Simon's first statement, bounded rationality was to be a theory that took account of neurophysiological and linguistic limits on the solving of complex problems. Twenty years later Williamson gives the theme a new direction by considering the problem-solving, decision-making, information-coding functions of institutions. The rational individual does not need to take all factors into account. Some of the environment is inside his skin. The internal organization of an institution provides a way of economizing in cognitive effort (Williamson 1975). Williamson works out the steps by which the costs of transactions would indicate to the rational agent whether it will pay off best to remain within a free competitive market environment or to accept a contract of employment and enter a bureaucratic environment. Based on transaction costs he proposes a model of the evolution of social forms. Further steps toward an economic analysis of institutions result in a theoretical scheme in which the rational agent is assumed to be making choices among social forms for the one best adapted to his interests in a given environment. With other rational agents he will be developing conventions to solve coordination problems. Finally, the institution (which in this analysis is defined as the conventions which it pays to observe) depends on securing compliance from fellows (Schelling 1960; Lewis 1969; Schotter 1981). Our attention must eventually turn toward the invention of low-cost compliance-seeking devices. At this point the risks from nature become very interesting for their system-maintaining uses.

In chapter 5 we contrasted two attitudes to natural disasters. One is opportunist in claiming political credit for disasters instead of pinning blame for them on disapproved deviants. This is found in a type of society which calls its members to heroism for the sake of great honors and rewards. This regime does not need to invent additional compliance-securing devices: It works because (and only if) it provides valued individual incentives. The other type, which we called hierarchy, needs to make clear to members at all times that they can best secure their private inter-

ests by conformity. This is the type of society in which anticipated natural disasters pencil a firm underlining of essential conventions. Each regime animadverts differently at post mortems,
inquests, and other inquiries into disaster.

First, the heroic, adversarial society reinforces dramatically its
own appropriate idea of its own just society. Its neutral cosmos
and belief in powerful personal weaponry direct attention to
where power is actually located. Power is not veiled or frustrated
in such a regime and the cosmological theory gives it only such
legitimation as it needs to bring heroes and their followings to
open confrontation. The focus on disaster triggers inquiries which
trace the real distribution of power and its challengers. It creates
plausibility structures which legitimate both the society and its
particular view of risk.

Second, the hierarchy uses the moral cosmos to uphold authority and to channel power to legitimate office holders. By attributing deaths and accidents of all kinds to nature (and sometimes to
the dead), live officeholders evade the unpopularity of meting out
punishment.

This approach to different patterns of risk perception relates it
to types of legitimating procedures in different social environments. For it to be plausible to other social scientists, several
things more are needed. On the empirical side a careful ethnog-
raphy is needed of what is said and done about disasters before
and after they happen. A meticulous assessment of community
structures within a typology of institutions needs to be worked
out. On the theoretical side, the topic of latent functions could be
revived and revised. This conception was important in the 1950s
when Robert Merton (1968a) used it to contrast with the manifest
function of an organization. Manifest are the functions which the
social unit is instituted expressly to perform and on whose performance it is judged. The hidden or latent functions are those
which seem to be unbudgeted: the sociability of members, the
protection of their status, the growth of solidarity as they work together, and the definition of their social boundaries. Latent functions were relegated to a secondary theoretical importance, even
before functionalism came under criticism in the 1960s, probably
because they are by definition difficult to observe. But there
seems to be a trade-off worth exploring between the concepts of
latent and manifest social goals in connection with risk acceptability.

94

It seems reasonable to claim that the more directly members are rewarded individually for their performance of their manifest roles in an organization, the less they will try to draw one another's energies into latent activities that maintain the organization in being. Vice versa, the smaller the rewards for working in the manifest role system, the more effort will be expended on indirect mutual reinforcement and persuasion. For example, this type of individualist society makes immediate direct payoffs to its successful heroes; in the hierarchy, payments are slow and obliquely related to individual input. In the former case, it is likely that there will be less harnessing of risks from nature to strengthen the collectivity. In the latter case, consensus about the needs of the collectivity will give credibility to blame-pinning. Husbands as a category will stand together to support allegations that a wife's adultery kills babies; the category of fathers will support belief in the power of the paternal curse; but neither will make their accusations credible unless they have the moral support of the community at large. Moral support is hardly enough in itself. The weaker the collectivity's power to reward its loyal members, the thicker the conceptual screen that identifies natural risks and relates them to disloyalty.

To develop this approach we turn to a form of social life which depends least upon material rewards for its members: the voluntary association. As usually described by sociologists it is a double hybrid. Other organizations are defined by their specific functions (market, bureaucracy), but this is more a form of community life. The full sense of the term community is a committed group in which individuals derive their life support and which bounds their commitments. The voluntary association seems to be an embryonic, partial, or unfulfilled attempt at creating community—it is an association whose members are often able to boast more of having kept together than of having achieved anything in particular over the years.

According to Tocqueville (1966), nothing else in America deserves so much attention as the widespread habit of forming voluntary associations. Though voluntary organization has been subsequently studied, little attention has been paid to the particular features which caught Tocqueville's eye. He posited a loose connection between associations and equality. He observed that associations are especially needful for mobilizing support in democratic societies, to make up for the absence of powerful private persons. He noted that if an association is to have any power in these conditions, it has to have a numerous membership. He also observed that this need to operate on a large scale poses difficulties. Though he seldom used the word "jealousy," he said much about the delusions, anonymity, and frustrations of competitive striving in a condition of general equality.

Tocqueville started from the general condition of equality in America compared with the aristocratic tradition of Europe. He argued that equality creates a power vacuum which naturally needs to be filled, so voluntary associations develop. The argument is stronger reversed. It better fits Tocqueville's views to start from a power vacuum and see that it creates problems of organization which are partly solved by adopting a principle of equality. For he clearly considered equality to be an uncomfortable position, full of discontent and lacking discipline. Equality means all being jumbled together in the same constantly fluctuating crowd, without recognition, honor, or social standing, eyes coveting small prizes and resenting small inequalities. "When everything is more or less level, the slightest variation is noticed. Hence, the more equal men are, the more insatiable will be their longing for inequality" (Tocqueville 1966:604). This is how he argued. He could have equally well expected that the experience of equality's disappointments might lead to instituted differences. If we were to ask Tocqueville why anybody should want to stay in that unhappy inchoate jumble, his answer would seem to invoke the positive value of equality, seen as a good in itself. The benefit of equality must outweigh its disadvantages.

A very different approach to the question of why some people value equality so much can be found in Mancur Olson's *The Logic of Collective Action* (1965). This book suggests indirectly that people put up with the practical disadvantages of equality only under special circumstances. What he actually says is that according to rational choice theory, the voluntary organization that is not protected by coercive power and/or does not afford special selective benefits for its members will not succeed in creating a collective good and will experience grave organizational difficulties. Markets and hierarchies flourish, thanks to the rational expectation of members that they will gain individual, selective benefits. The less that individual selective benefits are available, the more the organization encounters problems of commitment, leadership, and decision-making. According to Olson, when there is no coercion and no selective individual benefit, a group is going to be bothered by free-rider problems. Each member will expect to be able to enjoy the public benefits created by the others without anyone noticing whether or not he puts in his bit. If there is a difference between big and small stake-holders, the latter will tend to blackmail the former, threatening to withdraw and so gaining a paralyzing veto power over the whole group. Leadership is thwarted; endless bargaining blocks the decisions of endless committees. Such a group has a problem even to raise funds for its minimum organization costs and must be judged to be especially fragile and especially vulnerable to internal dissension.

The first step this kind of organization needs to make when trying to collect contributions and prevent secessions is to draw a clear boundary around members against the outside world. Second, it will need to make a rule of 100 percent participation, so as to prevent any lazy member or newcomer from reaping unfair benefits. On this analysis, instead of starting with equality and moving to associations, we start with voluntary associations and see them forced by the absence of clear authority or incentives to institute equality as a control on free riders. Though this is as far as Olson takes us, it enables a great deal to be added to Tocqueville's insight.

We have seen how the morally punitive cosmos uses risk to uphold community, and how the neutral cosmos, harnessed to the conflict of individual heroes, uses risk to solve their followers' problems of allegiance—in each case, the response to misfortune is incorporated into the institutional structure and used to solve different organizational problems. The voluntary association has even more severe difficulties in committing its members than does the hierarchy. Consequently, it persists only if it can develop a certain characteristic response to news of disaster. Voluntary organization works better than Olson thinks because of its use of the idea of the cosmic plot and its strategy of impeachment.

Cosmic Plot in Central Africa

Voluntariness of association can be treated as a dimension of any social unit. In Central Africa during the colonial period, the administrative officers reported over and over again the highly fissile nature of the societies they were governing. Villages no longer

97

threatened by marauders or organized for long-distance trade tended to split and spread; any leader's ambition to hold his village together was periodically and regularly thwarted. Without being voluntary associations, these communities had the same organizational troubles as Olson's theory predicts and for the same reasons. The villages shifted their sites every decade or so. The power had gone out of the political system. No fixed land rights were maintained in the slash and burn cultivation; tsetse fly would kill livestock. So there was nothing to inherit and nothing else to attract the footloose to choose to stay in one village rather than in another. The active young men were apt to use the threat of withdrawal effectively to get forgiveness for any misdeeds. Always the shared belief that it is good to live in a stable united village was strained by quarrels which burst into general conflagration after a succession of misfortunes had caused a witch to be identified in their midst. The alleged witch's friends would find themselves in a faction counterpoised against the accusers. The quarrels would have been festering over decades until solution by the exile of the witch or the splitting of the village. The villagers used the accusation of witchcraft and the threat of distant conspiracy to solve their own organizational problems. For a summary of the literature on which this discussion is based, see the following examples of a sustained tradition of inquiry: Gluckman et al. (1949); Mitchell (1956); Middletown and Winter (1983); Douglas (1970).

The voluntary organization is committed, by internal political needs, to make a virtue of equality. It will be led by the weight of individual strategies to associate any signs of personal ambition with inequality, corruption, social stratification, and the inhumane machinations of the outside world. So long as there are no internal crises, commitment to equality within a closed group is enough to promote latent intentions that the voluntary organization should survive. But this type of organization is prone to factionalism. Faction leaders are a threat; one way to control them is to accuse them of treacherous alliance with the bad outside world. The more the internal crises heat up, the more it suits the latent goals of the organization for everyone committed to it to find on the horizon signs of conspiracy and disaster which can be staved off only by stamping out the factions. When confrontation cannot be avoided, the perceived dangers justify impeaching and expelling the disruptive faction leader. (This applies not only to voluntary associations but to any group unable to coerce or to provide selective benefits for its individual members.) One function of the impeached traitor in the sect-like association is to explain its failure to produce the promised collective good—it is all his fault. A second function is to slow down the process of fission by holding up the awful warning of the convicted evildoer. Another function is to provide an idiom for absolving the duty of obedience so as to legitimate fission when it must come.

This argument claims that the organizations which are most keenly alert to low-probability, high-consequence danger are religious sects and communes (notoriously millennialist and apt to prophesy doom) and also any political lobbies, new political movements, and public interest groups not able to provide special selective benefits for their members. The more difficulty they have in holding their membership together and getting common dues paid, the more they are tempted to invoke cosmic plot and to impeach a traitor. The doom-laden cosmos is part of the functioning of an organizational type whose latent goals present a particularly acute problem.

This general argument is offered as an approach to the question of how humans ever perceive and take account of low probabilities: In general they do not; unless institutions are focused in that direction, they never would. Their field of attention is held to the middle ground. Social pressures hold it there. Social pressures filter the interpretation of the world's events. But societies come in various forms: They meet their organizational problems in different ways; they have different opportunities. In a complex society, the mix of individual competition, hierarchy, and voluntary associations will determine the mix of attention to imminent prospects of man-made and natural disasters. Contrary to what is often alleged, the issue has little to do with the amount of exploitation and injustice rampant in the society at large. It concerns the coding of information in the internal organization of institutions. The case that is being argued here is strengthened by psychologists who ponder how real world probabilities are formed in the minds of individuals.

The distinction between objective (or mathematical) probability and subjective (or psychological) probability has always been important in risk analysis. People do not consistently make the choices that will maximize their expected winnings or minimize their expected losses, even though there is reason to assume that they have these goals. Such a discrepancy is often treated as a cognitive weakness. Ward Edwards (1953) discovered that individuals have marked preferences for some probabilities over others. We could assume that this is due to quirky unreasonableness. But the decision-maker may be trying to exploit his own

99

quite confident knowledge about how probabilities and payoffs are correlated in the world outside the laboratory test situation. A big win is always more surprising than a small win. As Edwards says: "High positive or negative payoffs are typically associated with low probabilities, while mediocre or zero payoffs are typically associated with high probabilities. This, I assert, is simply a fact about the world in which we live" (1954). Lola Lopes (1981) has made the point that in the real world individuals cannot expect to play any game through the long run of probabilities. Long-run arguments should not be applied to decisions about short-run outcomes.

> The problem is not simply that decisions must sometimes be made about "gambles" to be "played" only once. Rather, the more fundamental problem is that whatever policy the person adopts for managing the myriad of risky operations that come along, that policy must "pay off" within the finite time span before one's stake—or one's life—runs out.

One can suppose that an established habit of finding that life is made of short-run decisions will be part of the cognitive equipment that the individual takes with him into the test situation. And one can suppose that other habits of thought are equally deep-rooted and equally influenced by the institutional environment.

> There is probably no psychological process more fundamental to individual survival than the ability to do induction. And there is no part of the inductive process that we know less about than how it begins. What makes us notice some things and not others? And how are the things we do notice linked to the hypotheses we generate about the world? [Lopes 1982]

Thinking about the real world probabilities which experimental subjects bring with them into the psychological laboratory and no doubt use for their answers to questions about choice leads us to the basic issues about the foundations of probability outlined in Arrow's 1951 essay "Alternative Approaches to the Theory of Choice in Risk-Taking Situations" (referred to in chapter 4). It is no part of this report to enter that subject. But skirting it gingerly, it is necessary to remind the risk analysts of Durkheim's contention that ideas about the world come directly out of social experience. So ideas about the randomness and connectedness of events are not independent. Ideas about the short run, how short it is, and ideas about the connection between probabilities and payoffs can be traced to commitments to kinds of social organization and to the kinds of experiences and kinds of interpretations current in them.

Bibliography

Adorno, T. W., ed. 1950. *Authoritarian Personality,* American Jewish Committee Social Studies Series Publication #3. New York: Harper.

Ainsworth, M. D. 1962. "The Effect of Maternal Deprivation: A Review of Findings and Controversy in the Context of Research Strategy." In *Deprivation of Maternal Care: A Reassessment of Its Effects.* Edited by M. D. Ainsworth. Public Health Papers 13. Geneva; World Health Organization.

Alexander, Richard. 1979. "Evolution and Culture." In *Evolutionary Biology and Human Social Behavior.* Edited by N. Chagnon and W. Irons. North Scituate, Mass.: Duxbury.

Allais, Maurice. 1953. "Le Comportement de l'homme rationnel devant le risque; Critique des postulats et axiomes de l'école Americaine." *Econometrica* 21:503-46.

———, and Hagen, O., eds. 1979. *Expected Utility Theory and the Allais Paradox: Contemporary Discussions of Decisions Under Uncertainty with Allais's Rejoinder.* Netherlands: Reidel.

Allison, Graham T. 1971. *The Essence of Decision: Explaining the Cuban Missile Crisis.* Boston: Little, Brown.

Allport, Gordon W., and Postman, Leo. 1947. *The Psychology of Rumor.* London: Russell and Russell.

Almond, S. A., and Verba, S. 1963. *The Civic Culture: Political Attitudes and Democracy in Five Nations.* Princeton, N. J.: Princeton University Press.

———, eds. 1980. *The Civic Culture Revisited.* Boston: Little, Brown.

Amihud, Yakov. 1979. "Critical Examination of the New Foundations of Utility." In Allais and Hagan.

Arrow, Kenneth. 1951. "Alternative Approaches to the Theory of Choice in Risk-Taking Situations." *Econometrica* 19:404–37.

Ashby, Eric, and Anderson, Mary. 1981. *The Politics of Clean Air*. Oxford: Clarendon Press.

Back, K. W., and Gergen, K. J. 1963. "Apocalyptic and Serial Time Orientations and the Structure of Opinions. *Public Opinion Quarterly* 27:427–42.

Balkin, Steven. 1979. "Victimization Rates Safety and Fear of Crime." *Social Problems* 26:343–58.

Barber, Bernard. 1961. "Resistance by Scientists to Scientific Discovery." *Science* 134:596–602.

Barlett, Peggy, ed. 1980. *Agricultural Decision-Making: Anthropological Contributions to Rural Development*. New York: Academic Press.

Barry, Brian, and Hardin, Russell, eds. 1982. *Rational Man and Irrational Society*. Berkeley, Calif.: Sage.

Barry, Brian, and Sikora, Dick. 1978. *Obligations to Future Generations*. Philadelphia: Temple University Press.

Ben-David, Shaul; Kneeze, Allen V.; and Schulze, W. D. 1979. "A Study of the Ethical Foundations of Benefit-Cost Analysis Techniques." Working paper, Department of Economics, University of New Mexico.

Berger, Peter L. 1969a. *The Sacred Canopy*. New York: Doubleday.

———. 1969b. *The Social Reality of Religion*. London: Faber & Faber.

———, and Luckmann, Thomas. 1966. *The Social Construction of Reality: A Treatise in the Sociology of Knowledge*. New York: Doubleday.

Bernoulli, Daniel. 1738. "Exposition of a New Theory on the Measurement of Risk." Translated by Louise Sommer. Translation published in *Econometrica* 22:23–36.

Bernstein, Basil. 1971. *Theoretical Studies Towards a Sociology of Language. Class, Codes and Control, vol. 1*. London: Routledge & Kegan Paul.

———. 1973. *Applied Studies Towards a Sociology of Language. Class, Codes and Control, vol. 2*. London: Routledge & Kegan Paul.

———. 1975. *Towards a Theory of Educational Transmission. Class, Codes and Control, vol. 3*. London: Routledge & Kegan Paul.

Boltanski, Luc. 1970. "Taxinomies populaires, taxinomies savantes: Les Objects de la Consommation et leur classement." *Revue Française de Sociologie* 11:33–34.

Boswell, D. M. 1969. "Personal Crises and the Mobilization of the Social Network." In *Social Networks in Urban Situations: Analyses of Personal Relationships in Central African Towns*. Edited by J. C. Mitchell. Manchester University Press.

Bowlby, J. 1951. *Maternal Care and Mental Health*. Geneva: World Health Organization.

Breen, T. H., and Innes, Stephen. 1980. *Myne Own Ground: Race and Freedom on Virginia's Eastern Shore, 1640–1676*. New York: Oxford University Press.

Brown, George; Bhrolchain, M. N.; and Harris, T. 1975. "Social Class and Psychiatric Disorder Among Women in an Urban Population." *Sociology* 9:225–54.

Brown, Roger. 1965. *Social Psychology*. New York: Free Press.

Buckner, H. Taylor. 1965. "A Theory of Rumor Transmission." *Public Opinion Quarterly* 29:54–70.

Burton, I.; Kates, R. W.; and White, G. F. 1978. *The Environment as Hazard*. New York: Oxford University Press.

Calabresi, Guido. 1970. *The Costs of Accidents*. New Haven: Yale University Press.

Campbell, Donald. 1975. "On the Conflicts Between Biological and Social Evolution and Between Psychology and Moral Tradition." *American Psychologist* 30:1103–26.

Campbell, T. Colin. 1980. "Chemical Carcinogens and Human Risk Assent." Special articles in *Federation Proceedings* 39:2467–84.

Cancian, Frank. 1967. "Stratification and Risk-Taking: A Theory Tested on Agricultural Innovations." *American Sociological Review* 32:912–27.

———. 1972. *Change and Uncertainty in a Peasant Economy: The Maya Corn Farmers of Zinacantan.* Stanford, Calif.: Stanford University Press.

Caplow, Theodore. 1947. "Rumors in War." *Social Forces* 25:298–302.

Carlson, J. L., and Davis, C. M. 1971. "Cultural Values and the Risky-Shift." *Journal of Personality and Social Psychology* 20:392–99.

Carter, Luther J. 1979. "Dispute Over Cancer Risk Quantification." *Science* 203:1324–25.

Chamberlin, John. 1982. "Provision of Collective Goods as a Function of Group Size." In Barry and Hardin.

Clark, W. 1977. "Managing the Unknown: An Ecological View of Risk Assessment." In Kates.

Cohen, Jonathan. 1981. "Can Human Irrationality Be Experimentally Demonstrated?" *Behavioral and Brain Sciences* 4:317–70.

Coleman, James; Katz, Elihu; and Menzel, A. 1962. "The Diffusion of an Innovation Among Physicians." *Sociometry* 20:253–70.

Crandall, Robert W., and Lave, Lester B., ed. 1981. *The Scientific Basis of Health and Safety Regulations: Studies in the Regulation of Economic Activity.* Washington, D. C.: Brookings Institution.

Dahrendorf, Ralf. 1979. *Life Chances.* London: Weidenfeld & Nicolson.

Deutsch, Elizabeth. 1982. "W. I. C. and the Vendors." Research Report, Center for Health Services and Policy Research, Northwestern University.

Dion, K. L.; Baren, R. S.; and Miller, N. 1971. "Why Do Groups Make Riskier Decisions Than Individuals?" In *Experimental Social Psychology*, vol. 5. Edited by L. Berkowitz. New York: Academic Press.

Donzelot, V. J. 1979. *The Policing of Families.* New York: Pantheon Books.

Douglas, James. 1983. "How Actual Political Systems Cope with the Paradoxes of Social Choice." In *Social Choice and Cultural Bias.* Collaborative Paper 83. Laxemburg, Austria: International Institute for Applied Systems Analysis.

———; Douglas, Mary; and Thompson, Michael. 1983. "Social Choice and Cultural Bias: A Collaborative Paper." Laxemburg, Austria: International Institute for Applied Systems Analysis.

Douglas, Mary. 1966. *Purity and Danger; An Analysis of Concepts of Pollution and Taboo.* London: Routledge & Kegan Paul.

———. 1975. "Couvade and Menstruation." In *Implicit Meanings: Essays in Anthropology.* London: Routledge & Kegan Paul. Originally published as "The Relevance of Tribal Studies." *Journal of Psychosomatic Research* 15 (1971):60–72.

———. 1978. "Cultural Bias." Occasional paper 35, Royal Anthropological Institute. Republished in *In the Active Voice.* London: Routledge & Kegan Paul.

———, ed. 1970. *Witchcraft Confessions and Accusations.* Association of Social Anthropologists, vol. 9. London: Tavistock.

———. 1982. *Essays in the Sociology of Perception.* London: Routledge & Kegan Paul.

———. 1984. *Food in the Social Order.* New York: Basic Books.

Douglas, Mary, and Gross, Jonathan. 1981. "Food and Culture: Measuring the Intricacy of Rule Systems." *Social Science Information* 20:1–35.

Douglas, Mary, and Isherwood, Bryan. 1978. *The World of Goods: An Anthropological Approach to the Theory of Consumption*. New York: Basic Books.

Douglas, Mary, and Wildavsky, Aaron. 1982. *Risk and Culture; An Essay on the Selection of Technological and Environmental Dangers*. Berkeley: University of California Press.

Downes, David M. 1976. *Gambling, Work and Leisure: A Study Across Three Areas*. London: Routledge & Kegan Paul.

Durkheim, Émile, 1933. [1893]. *The Division of Labour in Society*. New York: Free Press.

———. 1952. *Suicide: A Study in Sociology*. Edited by George Simpson. London: Routledge & Kegan Paul.

Edwards, Ward. 1953. "Probability Preferences in Gambling." *American Journal of Psychology* 66:349–64.

———. 1954. "The Theory of Decision-Making." *Psychological Bulletin* 51:380–417.

Efron, Edith. 1984. *The Apocalyptics, Cancer and the Big Lie; How Environmental Politics Controls What We Know About Cancer*. New York: Simon and Schuster.

Evans-Pritchard, E. 1937. *Witchcraft, Oracles, and Magic Among the Azande*. Oxford: Clarendon Press.

———. 1956. *Nuer Religion*. Oxford: Clarendon Press.

Farmer, F. R. 1981. "Quantification of Physical and Engineering Risks." *Proceedings of the Royal Society* (London) A376:103–19.

Festinger, Leon, et al. 1948. "A Study of a Rumor: Its Origin and Spread," *Human Relations* 1:464–86.

Fischhoff, B.; Hohenemser, C.; Kasperson, R.; and Kates, R. W. 1978. "Handling Hazards." *Environment* 20:16–37.

Fischhoff, B.; Lichtenstein, S.; Slovic, P.; Keeney, R.; and Derby, S. 1980. *Approaches to Acceptable Risk: A Critical Guide*. Oak Ridge National Laboratory for U. S. Nuclear Regulatory Commission. Washington, D. C.: U. S. Government Printing Office.

Foucault, Michel. 1970. [1966]. *The Order of Things: An Archaeology of the Human Sciences*. Translated from *Les Mots et les choses*. New York: Pantheon Books.

Fox, Renee C. 1980. "The Evolution of Medical Uncertainty." *Health and Society* 58:1–49.

Frankel-Brunswick, Egon. 1948. "Dynamic and Cognitive Categorization of Qualitative Material: Interviews of the Ethnically Prejudiced." *Journal of Psychology* 25:261–77.

———. 1949. "Intolerance of Ambiguity as an Emotional and Perceptual Personality Variable." *Journal of Psychology* 18:108–43.

———. 1954. "Psychoanalysis and the Unity of Science." *Proceedings of the American Academy of Arts and Sciences* 80:273–347.

Frazer, C., et al. 1970. "Risky Shifts, Cautious Shifts and Group Polarization." *European Journal of Social Psychology* 1:7–30.

Fried, Charles. 1970. *An Anatomy of Values*. Cambridge, Mass.: Harvard University Press.

Friedman, M. 1957. *A Theory of the Consumption Function*. New York: National Bureau of Economic Research, Plenum.

———, and Savage, L. J. 1948. "The Utility Analysis of Choices Involving Risk." *Journal of Political Economy* 56:279–304.

Garcia, R. 1982. *Nature Pleads Not Guilty.* New York: Pergamon Press.

Garofalo, James. 1979. "Victimization and the Fear of Crime." *Journal of Research in Crime and Delinquency* 1979:80–97.

Gartrell, J. W. 1972. "Status, Inequality and Innovation." *American Sociological Review* 7:318–37.

———. 1973. "Curvilinear and Linear Models Relating Status and Innovative Behavior." *Rural Sociology* 38:391–411.

Gellner, Ernest. 1962. "Concepts and Society." *Transactions of 5th World Congress of Sociology* 1:153–83. Reprinted in B. Wilson, ed. Oxford: Blackwells.

———. 1969. *Saints of the Atlas.* London: Weidenfeld & Nicolson.

Gergen, K. J., and Gergen, Mary M. 1973. "Explaining Human Conduct: Form and Function." In *Conceptual Issues in the Human Sciences.* Berkeley, Calif.: Sage.

———. 1982. *Toward Transformation in Social Knowledge.* New York: Springer-Verlag.

Gladwin, Christine. 1975. "A Model of the Supply of Smoked Fish from Cape Coast to Kumasi." In *Formal Methods in Economic Anthropology.* Edited by C. Gladwin and S. Plattes. Washington, D. C.: American Anthropological Association.

———. 1980. "A Theory of Real-Life Choice: Applications to Agricultural Decisions." In *Agricultural Decision-Making: Anthropological Contributions to Rural Development.* Edited by Peggy Barlett. New York: Academic Press.

Gluckman, Max; Barnes, John; and Mitchell, Clyde. 1949. "The Village Headman in British Central Africa." *Africa* 19:89–106.

Gorovitz, Samuel. 1979. "The St. Petersburg Puzzle." In Allais and Hagen.

Golding, M. P. 1972. "Obligations to Future Generations." *Monist.* 56:85–99.

Gould, Stephen Jay. 1981. *The Mismeasure of Man.* New York: Norton.

Graham, Julie, and Shakow, Don. 1981. "Risk and Reward: Hazard Pay for Workers." *Environment* 23:14–20, 44–45.

Green, Colin H. 1980. "Risk: Beliefs and Attitudes." In *Fires and Human Behavior.* Edited by D. Cantor. New York: Wiley.

———, and Brown, R. A. 1980. "Through a Glass Darkly: Perceiving Perceived Risks to Health and Safety." Prepared for the Workshop on Perceived Risk, Eugene, Oregon, Central Directorate on Environmental Pollution.

———. 1981a. "The Accuracy of Beliefs About Risk." *Atom* 295:129–31.

———. 1981b. "The Perception and Acceptability of Risk—A Summary of the Results of Work Conducted Under Contracts." Working Paper, Research Unit, School of Architecture, Duncan of Jordanstone College of Art, Dundee, Scotland.

Gross, Jonathan, and Rayner, Steve. 1985. *Measuring Culture: A Paradigm for the Analysis of Social Organization.*

Guedeney, C., and Mendel G. 1973. *L'Angoisse Atomique et Les Centres Nucléaires.* Paris: Payot.

Gusfield, Joseph R. 1981. *The Culture of Public Problems: Drinking, Driving and the Symbolic Order.* Chicago: University of Chicago Press.

Hacking, Ian. 1975. *The Emergence of Probability: A Philosophical Study of Early Ideas About Probability, Induction and Statistical Inference.* Cambridge: Cambridge University Press.

Hamilton, V., and Warburton, D., eds. *Human Stress and Cognition: An Information Processing Approach.* New York: Wiley.

Harvey, M. 1979. *Project Summary: Improving the Societal Management of Technological Hazards*. Eugene, Ore.: Clark University Center for Technology, and Decision Research, a Branch of Perceptronics.

Hebb, Donald O. 1949. *The Organization of Behavior: A Neuro-psychological Theory*. New York: Wiley.

Heberlein, Thomas, A., and Black, J. Stanley. 1981. "Cognitive Consistency and Environmental Action." *Environment and Behavior* 13:717–34.

Heider, Fritz. 1958. *The Psychology of Interpersonal Relations*. New York: Wiley.

Henderson, L. J. 1935. "The Patient and Physician as a Social System." *New England Journal of Medicine* 212:819–23.

Hicks, John. 1962. "Safety First and the Holding of Assets." *Econometrica* 4:310–90.

Hogarth, Robin M. 1980. *Judgment and Choice: The Psychology of Decision*. New York: Wiley.

———. 1981. "Decision-Making in Organizations and the Organization of Decision-Making." Uncompleted draft. Center for Decision Research, Graduate School of Business, University of Chicago.

Holdren, John P.; Smith, Kirk; and Morris, Gregory. 1979. Letter in *Science* 204:564–67.

Homans, George. 1950. *The Human Group*. New York: Harcourt, Brace.

Houthakker, H. S. 1957. "An International Comparison of Household Expenditure Patterns, Commemorating the Centenary of Engels Law." *Econometrica* 25:532–51.

Hume, David. 1888. [1739]. *A Treatise of Human Nature*. Edited by L. A. Selby-Bigge. Oxford: Oxford University Press.

Inhaber, Herbert. 1978. *Risk of Energy Production*. Ottawa, Canada: Atomic Energy Control Board.

———. 1979. "Risk with Energy from Conventional and Nonconventional Sources." *Science* 203:718–23.

Jantzen, J. M. 1978. *The Quest for Therapy in Lower Zaire*. Berkeley: University of California Press.

Jaspers, J. M. F., with Colin Fraser. 1981. "Attitudes and Social Representations." In *Social Representations*. Edited by S. Moscovici and R. Farr. Cambridge: Cambridge University Press.

Jones, E. E., and Davis, K. E. 1961. *Journal of Abnormal Psychology* 63:302–10.

Kahneman, Daniel and Tversky, Amos. 1973. "Availability: A Heuristic for Judging Frequency and Probability." *Cognitive Psychology* 5:207–32.

———. 1974. "Judgment Under Uncertainty: Heuristics and Biases." *Sciences* 185:1124–31.

———. 1979. "Prospect Theory: An Analysis of Decision Under Risk." *Econometrica* 47:263–90.

Kanter, Rosabeth Moss. 1972. *Commitment and Community: Communes and Utopias in Sociological Perspective*. Cambridge, Mass.: Harvard University Press.

Kasperson, Roger E. 1980. "The Dark Side of the Radio Active Waste Problem." In *Progress in Resource Management and Environmental Planning*, vol. 2. Edited by T. O. Riordan and K. Turner. New York: Wiley.

———, et al. 1980. "Public Opposition to Nuclear Energy: Retrospect and Prospect." *Science, Technology, and Human Values* 5:11–33.

Kates, Robert W. 1978. *Risk Assessment of Environmental Hazard*. New York: Wiley.

———, ed. 1977. *Managing Technological Hazard: Research Needs and Opportu-*

nities. Program on Technology, Environment and Man, Monograph 25, Institute of Behavioral Science, Boulder, Colorado.

Keagan, John. 1976. *The Face of Battle.* New York: Viking Press.

Kemeny, John G. 1979. *The Report of the President's Commission on the Accident at Three Mile Island.* Washington, D. C.: U.S. Government Printing Office.

Knott, Jack. 1982. "Incremental Theory and the Regulation of Risk." Paper presented at the annual meeting of the American Political Science Association, Denver.

Krantz, David H.; Fong, Godfrey T.; and Nisbett, Richard E. 1983. "Formal Training Improves the Application of Statistical Heuristics to Everyday Problems." Report issued from the Institute for Social Research, University of Michigan, Ann Arbor.

Kunreuther, Howard, and Wright, Gavin. 1979. "Safety First, Gambling, and the Subsistence Farmer." In Roumasset, et al.

Kunreuther, Howard, *et al.* 1978. *Disaster Insurance Protection: Public Policy Lessons.* New York: Wiley.

Lalonde, Marc. 1974. *A New Perspective on the Health of Canadians: A Working Document.* Ottawa: Ministry of National Health and Welfare, Government of Canada.

La Porte, Todd R., ed. 1975. *Organized Social Complexity: Challenge to Politics and Policy.* Princeton, N. J.: Princeton University Press.

Lave, L. B., and Romer, T. 1983. "Specifying Risk Goals: Inherent Problems with Democratic Institutions." *Risk Analysis* 3:217–27.

Lawless, E. 1974. *Technology and Social Shock—100 Cases of Public Concern Over Technology.* Kansas City, Mo.: Midwest Research Institute.

Lee, T. R. 1981. "Perception of Risk: The Public's Perception of Risk and the Question of Irrationality." *Proceedings of the Royal Society* (London) A376:5–16.

Leontiev, W. L. 1947. "The Internal Structure of Functional Relationships." *Econometrica* 15:361–73.

Levi, Isaac. 1980. *The Enterprise of Knowledge: An Essay on Knowledge Credal Probability and Choice.* Appendix. Cambridge, Mass.: MIT Press.

Lévy Bruhl, Lucian. 1966. [1910]. *How Natives Think.* New York: Washington Square Press. Translated from *Les Fonctions mentales dans les sociétés inferieures.*

Lewis, Charles. 1982. "Giving Birth: Fathers at Delivery." In *Fatherhood: Pschological Aspects,* edited by N. Beail and J. McGuire. London: Junction Books.

Lewis, David. 1969. *Convention: A Philosophical Study.* Cambridge, Mass.: Harvard University Press.

Lindblom, Charles. 1959. "The Science of Muddling Through." *Public Administration Review* 19:78–88.

———. 1965. *The Intelligence of Democracy.* New York: Free Press.

———. 1979. "Still Muddling: Not Yet Through." *Public Administration Review* 39: 517–27.

Loftus, Elizabeth. 1980. *Memory: Surprising New Insights Into How We Remember and Why We Forget.* Reading, Mass.: Addison-Wesley.

Logan, R., and Nelkin, D. 1980. "Labor and Nuclear Power." *Environment* 22:6–13.

Lopes, Lola. 1981. "Notes, Comments, and New Findings: Decision-making in the Short Run." *Journal of Experimental Psychology* 7:377–85.

109

————. 1982. "Doing the Impossible: A Note on Induction and the Experience of Randomness." *Journal of Experimental Psychology* 8:626–36.

Lowrance, W. W. 1976. *Of Acceptable Risk: Science and the Determination of Safety*. Los Altos, Calif.: William Kaufmann.

MacLean, Douglas. 1982. "Risk and Consent: Philosophical Issues for Centralized Decisions." *Risk Analysis* 2:59–67.

March, J. G., and Simon, H. A. 1958. *Organizations*. New York: Wiley.

Mars, Gerald. 1982. *Cheats at Work*. London: Allen & Unwin.

Marshall, Alfred. 1890. *Principles of Economics*. Mathematical appendix. London: Macmillan.

Merton, Robert K. 1968a. "Manifest and Latent Functions: Toward the Codification of Functional Analysis in Sociology." In *Social Theory and Social Structure*, enlarged ed., New York: Free Press.

————. 1968b. "On the History and Systematics of Sociological Theory." In *Social Theory and Social Structure*, enlarged ed., New York: Free Press.

————, ed. 1973. *The Sociology of Science: Theoretical and Empirical Investigations*. Chicago: University of Chicago Press.

Middleton, John, and Winter, E. H., eds. 1983. *Witchcraft and Sorcery in East Africa*. London: Routledge & Kegan Paul.

Mitchell, Clyde. 1956. *The Yao Village*. Manchester: Manchester University Press.

Mitchell, Robert C. 1979. "Public Polling on Nuclear Power: A Critique of Post-Three Mile Island Polls." Discussion Paper D-61. Washington, D. C.: Resources for the Future.

————. 1980a. "How 'Soft', 'Deep', or 'Left'? Present Constituencies in the Environmental Movement for Certain World Views." *Natural Resources Journal* 20:345–58.

————. 1980b. "Public Opinion on Environmental Issues: Results of a National Public Opinion Survey." Washington, D. C.: Council on Environment Quality.

Morgan, Edmund S. 1975. *American Slavery-American Freedom: The Ordeal of Colonial Virginia*. New York: Norton.

Morin, Edgar. 1971. *Rumor in Orleans*. New York: Pantheon Books.

Morris, Louis A.; Mazis, Michael B.; and Barofsky, Ivan, eds. 1980. *Product Labelling and Health Risks*. Banbury Report, no. 6. Cold Spring Harbor, N. Y.: Cold Spring Harbor Laboratory.

Moscovici, S., and Zavalloni, M. 1969. "The Group as Polarizer of Attitudes." *Journal of Personality and Social Psychology* 12:125–35.

Myers, D. G., and Lamm, H. 1976. "The Group Polarization Phenomenon." *Psychological Bulletin* 83:602–27.

Nadel, Lynn. 1980. "Cognitive and Neural Maps." In *The Nature of Thought: Essays in Honor of D. O. Hebb*. Edited by P. W. Jusczyk and R. M. Klein. Hillsdale, N. J.: Laurence Erlbaum.

Nagel, Thomas. 1980. "The limits of objectivity." Tanner Lectures on Human Values, edited by S. M. McMurtin. University of Utah Press.

Naroll, R. S., and Von Bertalanffy, Ludwig. 1956. "The Principle of Allometry in Biology and the Social Sciences." *General Systems* 1:76–89.

NaVarro, V. 1975. "The Political Economy of Medical Care." *International Journal of Health Services* 5:65–94.

————. 1977. "Political Power, the State, and Their Implications in Medicine." *Review of Radical Political Economics* 9:61–80.

Nelkin, D. 1974. "Technological Decisions and Democracy: European Experiments in Public Participation." Berkeley, Calif.: Sage.

110

———. 1981a. "Some Social and Political Dimensions of Nuclear Power: Examples from Three Mile Island." *American Political Science Review* 75:132–42.

———. 1981b. "Nuclear Power as a Feminist Issue." *Environment* 23:14–20.

Nordhoy, F. 1962. *Group Interaction and Decision-Making Under Risk.* Unpublished master's thesis, School of Industrial Management, Massachusetts Institute of Technology.

Nozick, R. 1974. *Anarchy, State and Utopia.* New York: Basic Books.

Nuclear Regulatory Commission. 1975. *Reactor Safety Study: An Assessment of Accident Risks in U.S. Commercial Nuclear Power Plants.* Appendices 1 and 2. Washington, D. C.: Nuclear Regulatory Commission.

Olson, Mancur. 1965. *The Logic of Collective Action: Public Goods and the Theory of Groups.* Cambridge, Mass.: Harvard University Press.

O'Riordan, Timothy. 1982. "Risk Perception Studies and Policy Priorities." *Risk Analysis* 2:95–100.

Ortiz, Sutti. 1979. "The Effect of Risk Aversion Strategies on Subsistence and Cash Crop Decisions." In Roumasset et al.

———. 1980. "Forecasts, Decisions, and the Farmer's Response to Christian Environments." In Barlett.

Otway, Harry J., and Cohen J. J. 1975. "Revealed Preferences: Comments on the Starr Benefit-Risk Relationship." Laxemberg, Austria: International Institute for Applied Systems Analysis.

Otway, Harry J., and Thomas, Kerry. 1982. "Reflections on Risk Perception and Policy." *Risk Analysis* 2:69–81.

Ouchi, William G. L. 1980. "Markets, Bureaucracies and Clans." *Administrative Science Quarterly* 1:129–41.

Paige, K. E., and Paige, J. M. 1981. *The Politics of Reproductive Ritual.* Berkeley: University of California Press.

Piehler, Henry R.; Tverski, Aaron D.; Weinstein, Alvin S.; and Donaher, W. A. 1974. "Product Liability and the Technical Expert." *Science* 186:1089–93.

Plott, Charles. 1978. "On the Incorporation of Public Attitudes Towards Administrative Options." In *Risk Benefit Decisions and the Public Health.* Edited by J. A. Staffa. Proceedings of the Third FDA Science Symposium. Washington, D. C.: HEW, FDA.

Pruitt, D. G. 1971. "Choice Shifts in Group Discussion: An Introductory Review." *Journal of Personality and Social Psychology* 20:339–60.

Rawls, Joh. 1971. *Theory of Justice.* Cambridge, Mass.: Harvard University Press.

Roder, W. 1961. "Attitudes and Knowledge on the Topeka Flood Plain." In *Papers on Flood Problems.* Edited by G. F. White. Research paper 700, Department of Geography, University of Chicago.

Rogers, Everett M. 1982. *Diffusion of Innovation.* New York: Free Press.

———, and Shoemaker, F. F. 1971. *Communication of Innovations: A Cross-Cultural Approach.* New York: Free Press.

Rothman, Stanley, and Lichter, Robert S. 1982. "The Nuclear Energy Debate: Scientists, the Media and the Public." *Public Opinion,* August/September; pp. 47–52.

Rotter, J. B. 1966. "Generalized Expectancies for Internal Control Versus External Control of Reinforcements." *Psychological Monographs* 80:609.

Roumasset, James A.; Boussard, Jean-Marc; and Singh, Inderjit, eds. *Risk, Uncertainty and Agricultural Development.* New York: Agricultural Development Council.

Routley, R. 1979. "Nuclear Energy and Obligations to the Future." *Inquiry* 21:112–79.

111

Rowe, W. D. 1977. *An Anatomy of Risk*. New York: Wiley.

Roy, A. D. 1952. "Safety First and the Holding of Assets." *Econometrica* 20:431–449.

Sahlins, Marshall. 1974. *Stone Age Economics*. London: Tavistock.

Schelling, Thomas. 1960. *The Strategy of Conflict*. New York: Oxford University Press.

Schotter, Andrew. 1981. *The Economic Theory of Social Institutions*. Cambridge: Cambridge University Press.

Schrodt, Philip A. 1980. "The Political Impact of Risk." Unpublished paper.

Schulze, W. D., and Kneeze, A. V. 1981. "Risk in Cost-Benefit Analysis." *Risk Analysis* 1:81–88.

Schwartz, Thomas. 1979. "Welfare Judgments and Future Generations." *Theory and Decision* 11:181–94

Self, Peter. 1975. *Econocrats and the Policy Process: the Politics and Philosophy of Cost Benefit Analysis*. New York: Macmillan.

Selsnick, Philip. 1969. "Employees' Perspectives on Industrial Justice." In *Law, Society, and Industrial Justice*. New York: Russell Sage Foundation.

Sen, Amartya. 1970. *Collective Choice and Social Welfare*. Amsterdam: Elsevier.

———. 1977. "Starvation and Exchange Entitlements: A General Approach and Its Application to the Great Bengal Famine." *Cambridge Journal of Economics* 1:33–59.

———. 1981. *Poverty and Famines: An Essay on Entitlement and Deprivation*. Oxford: Clarendon Press.

Sewell, W. R. D. 1971. "Environmental Perceptions and Attitudes of Engineers and Public Health Officials." *Environment and Behavior* 3:23–60.

———. 1973. "Specialists, Laymen and the Process of Environmental Appraisal." *Regional Studies* 7:161–71.

Simon, Herbert. 1955. "A Behavioral Model of Rational Choice." *Quarterly Journal of Economics* 69:99–118.

———. 1979. *Models of Thought*. New Haven: Yale University Press.

Skultans, Vieda. 1975. *Madness and Morals: Ideas on Insanity in the 19th Century*. London: Routledge & Kegan Paul.

Slovic, Paul; Fischhoff, Baruch; and Lichtenstein, Sarah. 1979a. "Rating the Risks." *Environment* 21 (3):14–20.

———. 1979b. "Which Risks Are Acceptable?" *Environment* 21 (4):17–20.

———. 1980. In *Societal Risk Assessment: How Safe Is Safe Enough?* Edited by R. Schwing and W. A. Albers. New York: Plenum.

———. 1981. "Perceived Risk: Psychological Factors and Social Implications." *Proceedings of the Royal Society* (London) A376:17–34.

Slovic, Paul; Lichtenstein, Sarah; and Fischhoff, Baruch. 1979. "Images of Disaster: Perception and Acceptance of Risks from Nuclear Power." In *Energy Risk Management*. Edited by G. Goodman and W. Rowe. London: Academic Press.

Slovic, Paul, and Tversky, A. 1974. "Who Accepts Savage's Axiom?" *Behavioral Science* 19:368–72.

Smith, Michael D. 1979. "Hockey Violence: A Text of the Violence Sub-Culture Hypothesis." *Social Problems* 272:235–47.

Spangler, Miller B. 1980. "Syndromes of Risk and Environmental Protection: The Conflict of Individual and Societal Values." *Environmental Professional* 2:274–91.

———. 1981. "Risks and Psychic Costs of Alternative Energy Sources for Generating Electricity." *Energy Journal* 2:37–57.

Stallen, P. J. M., and Tomas, A. 1981. "Psychological Aspects of Risk: The Assessment of Threat and Control." Paper prepared for International School of Technological Risk Assessment, Erice-Sicily; Center for Technology and Policy Studies (TNO), Netherlands.

Starr, Chauncey. 1969. "Social Benefit Versus Technological Risk." *Science* 165:1232–38.

———. 1979. "Risk Benefit Analysis and Full Disclosure." Republished in *Current Issues in Energy*. New York: Pergamon Press.

Steinbruner, J. D. 1976. *The Cybernetic Theory of Decision*. Princeton, N. J.: Princeton University Press.

Stigler, George J. 1969. "The Development of Utility Theory." *Journal of Political Economy* 56:279–304.

———. 1975. *The Citizen and the State: Essays on Regulation*. Chicago: University of Chicago Press.

Stoner, J. A. 1961. "A Comparison of Individual and Group Decision, Involving Risk." Unpublished master's thesis, School of Industrial Management, Massachusetts Institute of Technology.

Strotz, R. H. 1957. "The Empirical Implications of a Utility Tree." *Econometrica* 25:269–80.

Thomas, Kerry. 1981. "Comparative Risks Perception: How the Public Perceives the Risks and Benefits of Energy Systems." *Proceedings of the Royal Society* (London) A376:35–50.

Thompson, Michael. 1982. "Among the Energy Tribes." Working paper 82–59. Laxemburg, Austria: International Institute for Applied Systems Analysis.

———. 1983. "Postscript: A Cultural Basis for Comparison." In *Risk Analysis and Decision Processes*, edited by H. Kunreuther, and J. Linnerooth. Berlin: Springer-Verlag.

———. 1980. "The Aesthetics of Risk: Culture or Contest." In *Societal Risk Assessment: How Safe Is Safe Enough?* Edited by R. C. Schwing and W. H. Albers. New York: General Motors Labs, Plenum.

Tocqueville, Alexis de. 1966. "Associations in Civil Life." In *Democracy in America*, vol. 2. Edited by J. P. Mayer and M. Lerner. New York: Harper & Row.

Torry, William I. 1979a. "Anthropological Studies in Hazardous Environments: Past Trends and New Horizons." *Current Anthropology* 30:517–40.

———. 1979b. "Hazards, Hazes, and Holes: A Critique of the *Environment as Hazard* and General Reflections on Disaster Research." *Canadian Geographer* 23:368–83.

———. 1982. "Distributive Justice Codes and Famine." Paper presented at the 81st annual meeting of the American Anthropological Association, Washington, D. C., December 4.

Trivers, Robert. 1972. "The Evolution of Reciprocal Altruism." *Quarterly Review of Biology* 46:35–57.

Tversky, A., and Kahneman, D. 1974. "Judgment Under Uncertainty: Heuristics and Biases: Biases in Judgements Reveal Some Heuristics of Thinking Under Uncertainty." *Science* 185:1124–31.

———. 1981. "The Framing of Decisions and the Psychology of Choice." *Science* 211:453–58.

U.S. Department of Health, Education, and Welfare. 1979. *Health of Minorities and Low Income Groups*. Public Health Service, Health Resources Administration, Office of Health Resources Opportunity. Washington, D. C.: U. S. Government Printing Office.

113

U.S. Department of Health and Human Services. 1980a. *Health of the Disadvantaged. Chart Book II.* Washington, D. C.: U. S. Government Printing Office.

————. 1980b. Vital Health Statistics Series 10. *Selected Health Characteristics by Occupation, U. S. 1975–76.* National Center for Health Statistics. Washington, D.C.: U. S. Government Printing Office.

————. 1983. *Health U. S.* Washington, D. C.: U. S. Government Printing Office.

Vogel, David. 1980. "Coercion Versus Consultation: A Comparison of Environmental Protection Policy in the U. S. and G. B." Paper presented to the British Politics Group, American Political Science Association annual convention.

Von Neumann, J., and Morgenstern, Oskar. 1953. *The Theory of Games and Economic Behavior.* Princeton, N. J.: Princeton University Press.

Wallach, M. A.; Kogan, N.; and Bem, D. J. 1962. "Group Influence on Individual Risk-Taking." *Journal of Abnormal and Social Psychology* 65:75–86.

————. 1974. "Diffusion of Responsibility and Level of Risk-Taking in Groups." *Journal of Abnormal and Social Psychology* 68:263–74.

Weinberg, Alvin. 1982. "Nuclear Safety and Public Acceptance." *Nuclear News* 25:54–58.

White, G. F. 1952. *Human Adjustment to Floods: A Geographical Approach to the Flood Problem in the U.S.* Research Paper 29, Department of Geography, University of Chicago.

Wildavsky, Aaron. 1975. *Budgeting: A Comparative Theory of Budgetary Processes.* Boston: Little, Brown.

————. 1984. *The Nursing Father: Moses as a Political Leader.* Tuscaloosa: University of Alabama Press.

Williams, Roger. 1980. *The Nuclear Power Decisions: British Policies, 1953–78.* London: Croom Helm.

Williamson, Oliver E. 1975. *Markets and Hierarchies: Analysis and Anti-Trust Implications.* New York: Free Press.

————. 1981. "Saccharin: An Economist's View." In Crandall and Lave.

Withey, Stephen. 1962. "Reaction to Uncertain Threat." In *Man and Society in Disaster.* Edited by G. W. Baker and D. W. Chapman. New York: Basic Books.

World Health Organization. 1978. *Environmental Health Criteria, Six: Principles and Methods for Evaluating the Toxicity of Chemicals,* pt. I. Geneva: World Health Organization.

Wynn, Briann. 1982a. "Institutional Mythologies and Dual Societies in the Management of Risk." In *The Risk Analysis Controversy: An Institutional Perspective,* edited by H. C. Kunreuther and E. V. Ley. Proceedings of a 1981 summer study on decision processes and institutional aspects of risk, International Institute for Applied Systems Analysis. Berlin: Springer-Verlag.

————. 1982b. *Rationality and Ritual: The Windscale Inquiry and Nuclear Decisions in Britain.* The British Society for the History of Science. Chalfont St. Giles, Bucks, England.

Zajonc, R. B.; Wolosin, A. A.; and Sherman, S. J. 1968. "Individual and Group Risk-Taking in a Two-Choice Situation." *Journal of Experimental Social Psychology* 4:89–107.

Zola, J. K. 1964. "Observations on Gambling in a Lower Class Setting." *Social Problems* 11:353–61.

Acknowledgments

I wish to thank the Russell Sage Foundation for its support of the initial stages of this research and Northwestern University for the very generous continued support, without which it would have been impossible. I thank also the International Institute for Applied Systems Analysis in Austria for helpful exposure to decision theory in 1981, the Social Science Research Council in England for bringing me to Oxford to consult with social psychologists in March 1982, and the Wenner Gren Foundation for supporting a visit to England and France in 1983–84.

Previous work with Aaron Wildavsky led me directly to these problems and my debt there is clear. Robert Merton's keen eye and sharp red pencil helped to shape the original research proposal. Thinking rationally about rationality is always very difficult, and, as usual, my husband helped me there.

In addition, kind colleagues have advised on parts of the text: Michael Thompson, Kenneth Friedman, Philip Schrodt, Barry Barnes, Constantine Zervos, Howard Kunreuther, David Edge, Lola Lopes, and Bruno Latour. I also thank Mary Anne Joseph and Anwar Ahadi for research assistance. Helen McFaul deserves special gratitude for skill and patience in putting the report together through numerous drafts. I am very grateful to Priscilla Lewis for editorial help and encouragement.

115